Tortured
for
His
Faith

Tortured for His Faith

by

HARALAN POPOV

An Epic of Christian Courage
and Heroism in Our Day

ZONDERVAN PUBLISHING HOUSE
A DIVISION OF THE ZONDERVAN CORPORATION
GRAND RAPIDS, MICHIGAN

TORTURED FOR HIS FAITH

Copyright © 1970 by Haralan Popov

Fourth printing	February 1971
Fifth printing	July 1971
Sixth printing	December 1971
Seventh printing	June 1972
Eighth printing	December 1972
Ninth printing	February 1973

Library of Congress Catalog Card Number: 77-102834

Printed in the United States of America

PREFACE

During 13 years and 2 months in Communist prisons, I was sustained by two things: First, the knowledge that my life was truly in God's hands, not the hands of my communist jailors; second, that I might live to someday give my testimony and tell what I witnessed. The purpose of this book is not to show man's depravity — which I experienced day and night for over 13 years — but rather to show *God's overwhelming love.* If anything should stand out in this book, let it be the overwhelming truth of *God's love* in the midst of man's *bestiality.*

In prison I learned the lesson of love as never before. Though I had preached of God's love from many pulpits, I came to see His love in a new way in the black despair of subterranean cells and in the faces of countless fellow-prisoners. Stripped of all material things and all distractions, I found a greater reality in God than I had ever known before. The truth often shines clearest where the circumstances are darkest.

I make no political attacks in this book, for I view communism not only as a political force but also as a "symptom" of a much deeper *spiritual sickness.* It is a "religion" of militant atheism. The inability to destroy faith in God is communism's "Achilles' heel." They desperately fear faith in God. Never were Paul's words more true than when he said, "We wrestle not against flesh and blood."

But I have another reason for writing this book. There are many false rumors abroad today that communism is "mellowing" toward religion and that the practices of the past, while bad, are over. I have been shocked to see how widely this communist deception is accepted. This is completely erroneous. Actually, Christianity is being attacked more severely behind the Iron Curtain today than ever before. Many still die in prisons.

Instead of trying to destroy the Church from *without,* in Russia and in other countries communism is subverting and controlling it from *within*. Instead of finishing the Church with one brutal blow, communism is now attempting to slowly strangle the Church bit by bit. The attack today is both more subtle and more dangerous.

Religion in communist lands is not free and open as some proclaim. Neither is it destroyed. It is alive and growing under persecution, as did the Early Church. In fact, an Underground Church has come alive in the Communist world. Its similarities with the Early Church are striking. It is to present my testimony and the story of the Underground Church that I write this book. I dedicate it to the thousands of our fellow-Christians who have died in prisons, many right alongside me, and to the body of Christ being tortured today in the communist world.

HARALAN POPOV

CONTENTS

At 4 in the morning on July 24, 1948, my doorbell suddenly started ringing insistently over and over. Sleepily I arose, put on my robe and went to the door. There stood three strangers, two of whom were in ordinary clothes and the other in a uniform. "We have come to search your house," the leader in civilian clothes said and pushed his way past me into the sleeping house. My wife Ruth heard the noise and joined me in the living room where we watched with bewilderment as the three men searched the entire house. As they were searching I thought, *It's finally come. The time is here at last.*

They searched everywhere — through books, beds, bookshelves, storage chests, drawers — for three hours. They didn't miss anything! As the sun came up around 7 a.m. they turned to me and ordered me to come along with them. I must come along but it was only for *"a little questioning,"* they explained.

Little did I know that this *"little questioning"* would last for thirteen endless years of torture and imprisonment. As they were shoving me out the door half-dressed, Rhoda, my little daughter awoke and came running into the living room. With a child's quick perception, she realized her father was being taken away. She burst into tears and began crying her little heart out — her body trembling and shaking from the sobbing.

"They're taking daddy. They're taking daddy!" she cried over and over.

The scene was just too much for me, and tears came into my eyes as I hugged Rhoda. Over and over I assured her I would be right back, though deep inside I knew this was the blow I had been expecting. But Rhoda's heart was broken in spite of all my assurances. She couldn't be consoled. I think that some-

9 •

how — in a child's own way — she knew she might never see her father again. With tears quietly brimming in my eyes I kissed Ruth and Rhoda good-by, knowing that I might never see them again.

Through all this my little son Paul slept and I never had a chance to say good-by to him. Ruth told me later she fell on her knees after we left and tearfully prayed that I would be returned before nightfall. After two or three hours she was visited by Pastor Manoloff's wife who told her that her husband had also been taken away.

Walking to the police station between the three men around 7 a.m., I held my head high. As the four-man "parade" walked down the street, I could feel the eyes of my friends, neighbors and church members on me. I knew that since my conversion I had served only God and I was in God's hands. From the depths of my heart I cried out to God, asking for His grace to endure whatever was before me.

At the police station I was searched from head to toe and then locked in a cell. Inside I found another man, an Armenian. The cell was filthy and littered with paper and rubbish. In one corner stood an old cracked clay pot which served as our "toilet." It was overflowing and the stench from it was terrible. I paced back and forth from 8 a.m. to 8 p.m., deeply concerned about Ruth, Rhoda and Paul.

THE ENDLESS NIGHTS BEGIN

At eight o'clock that evening, my cell door opened and a young man commanded me to accompany him. He took me down to the second floor to a beautifully furnished office where he introduced me to another young man. I was told he was to be addressed as "Mr. Inspector." I stood in front of "Mr. Inspector," and he fired his first question at me.

"Do you know the difference between the militia and the police?"

I thought the question was a joke, and said, "No, I don't. I have never been interested in such police matters." My reply irritated him and he shouted, "Don't play games with me, Prisoner Popov. Stand facing that wall and don't move!"

This sounds like a light punishment, but I can assure you it is most tiring and painful to the whole body, especially to the small of the back.

"Mr. Inspector" continued to ask me the same question from 8 p.m. to midnight as I stood stiffly. Every 5 or 10 minutes the question was repeated: "Do you know the difference between the militia and the police?" I tried to explain I didn't know. When I saw that I was getting nowhere I stopped answering. He screamed, "We'll teach you a lesson! Hold your arms straight up and don't move a muscle!"

Finally, around midnight, "Mr. Inspector" said, "I will tell you the difference between the militia and the police. Police are employed to guard the interests of the rich capitalists and the militia guards the interest of the honest working people." I was then allowed to lower my arms.

It was a hard "lesson" in communist semantics I had learned!

My arms felt as heavy as logs. I was then asked another question. "State just why you are here." I answered that three men had come to my home that morning and brought me there. I had been in a cell all day and no one had told me anything. "No," he replied, "you know why you are here."

"But I don't know for sure," I answered, though I had a very good idea.

After he had repeated the question for an hour, the "inspector" said, "I am going now. Stand there until morning. I'll return for your answer tomorrow morning and we'll see if you're any smarter by then."

He left me in the care of the young man named Jordan who had brought me from my cell. Jordan spent the night sitting in a chair behind me while I stood facing the wall. Little did I know ı was not only facing one night "at the wall," but would later be forced to stand for two weeks!

The last hours of the night between 3 and 7 a.m. were the most difficult. After standing with my face to the wall all night without a wink of sleep, these hours seemed as long as eternity. At last dawn came and Jordan took me back to the cell. The Armenian wanted to give me something to eat but I preferred to stretch out on the board bunk and rest. I was so tired I wanted only to sleep, but the swarming bedbugs and assorted other crawling things kept me awake. Before I knew it my body was covered with the creatures and it was impossible to sleep. I had to get up and pace back and forth. Later I heard rumor the cells were purposely infested with bedbugs, lice and vermin to make it worse for the prisoner. I never found out if this was true, but I suspect it was. There were armies of them.

It was now Sunday, July 25, and for the first time in many years I did not spend Sunday in a church. In my cell I knelt and my thoughts went out to my brothers and sisters in Christ who would be at worship at this moment. I prayed for my children and for my wife, whom I had left without money or food. How I would have loved to be with them! I asked the Lord to take care of them in the future whatever it held. I knew that the Great Persecution had begun for the sake of Christ. All down through Christian history this had happened again and again, and I prayed from deep within that God would give me strength to measure up to the disciples and martyrs of the Early Church. I surely couldn't do it on my own. A cricket sang from somewhere amongst the rotten floorboards of the cell block and my downtrodden soul was lifted up and my faith in God renewed.

The all-night interrogations continued for a week. The pattern was always the same. As soon as it was dark I was taken downstairs and made to stand exactly eight inches from the wall. There, from 7 p.m. until about 8 the next morning I was questioned and not permitted to close my eyes. If my eyes nodded, Jordan would leap up shouting, "Stop! Stop! That's not allowed." In the daytime I fought the swarming bedbugs so I had no chance to rest then either. No one was given any food in the prison, but my wife managed to find out where I was and sent food from home. I wanted desperately to see my family, to know how they were, but was not allowed to do so.

On Saturday night, no one came to take me downstairs. But around midnight I heard a key in the lock and an unfamiliar voice shouted, "Popov, get out here! You're being transferred."

I said good-by to the Armenian. We had become fast friends and I discovered in the year ahead close and true friendships developed between prisoners who shared common sufferings.

The police led me outside where a police car, commonly nicknamed "Black Raven," was waiting with two policemen in it. We drove off down the main street of Sofia and only minutes after we started we arrived at a big white building. It was the headquarters of the "DS" — the dreaded Secret Police.

"WELCOME TO THE WHITE HOUSE, PRISONER POPOV"

The Secret Police was called Dershavna Sigornost, or DS. It was headquartered in a large white building nicknamed by the people, "The White House." But I assure you this "White House" was very different from the American White House! Many of our country's finest men have gone into the "White House" and have never come out alive. It was rumored that the "White House" even had its own subterranean "graveyard" for disposal of bodies of its victims.

To the people of Bulgaria the name DS meant disappearance, suffering and death. Over one cell door was written a quotation from Dante's *The Divine Comedy*: "All hope abandon, ye who enter here." How

13 ●

appropriate! More people have died here than have come out alive, and those who survive do not live very long because of the torture to which they have been subjected. There was talk that people who passed the DS building could hear screams coming up through the cobblestone street from the sprawling complex of subterranean cells below. I later found out this was true.

When the "Black Raven" stopped and I was led into the building, fear and insecurity swept over me. It had been a week of sleeplessness and interrogation, and my body trembled and shook. As I was led through the door, the words from Psalm 73:28 came to me ". . . I have put my trust in the Lord God. . . ."

I knew I couldn't expect help from anyone else here in the "White House." I breathed a silent prayer, "God, my life is in Your hands." My fears began to melt away. I had a very strong feeling of peace. The tension in my body was gone. Death was perhaps waiting for me in the DS "White House," but my heart praised and worshiped the Lord.

When a man faces death, he examines himself and thinks of how he stands in relation with God. He sees things very clearly. I had resigned myself to the thought that my life on earth would soon be over and that within a short time I would be with the Lord. It was clear to me that I had been brought here to die. In the past week I had lost everything that was dear to me on earth — my wife, my family, my church, my home — but I felt God right beside me as I walked through the doors into the DS headquarters.

The guard looked at me mockingly and said, "Welcome to the White House, Prisoner Popov." Once more I was stripped and searched, then led upstairs to the third floor. Going up the stairs I noticed a wire net over the stairwell, put there so no prisoner could escape the DS by throwing himself over the stairs. Evidently so many prisoners had tried to commit suicide, this wire net had to be put up to catch them.

Up on the third floor, I was led down a long dark hallway, with grimy barred windows on one side and rows of rusty, dark cell doors on the other side. Each cell door had a little "Judas hole" with a sliding cover over it. These "Judas holes" allowed the guards to watch the prisoners. Barely audible moans came from the occupants of the cells. Guards had on thick cloth shoes so the prisoners couldn't hear their approach.

But let me tell you how I arrived at this point in my life. . . .

A "Hard-Core" Atheist Finds Christ

I was born and spent my youth in the beautiful little town of Krasno Gradiste, in Bulgaria. There were four of us children, three brothers and a sister. We were born in an old Turkish-built farmhouse, consisting of one room and a kitchen. The ceiling was so low that my father had to duck so as not to hit his head on the beams above. The house had a dirt floor, which mother painted with a mixture of manure, clay and water. It didn't smell very nice, but it was a disinfectant, and the manure kept the floor from cracking.

We all slept in one room, on the floor covered with rugs made of plaited reeds. On one side of the kitchen was the large, blackened fireplace on which stood an array of sooty, cracked clay pots. The beans which mother cooked for us in those days were as good as the daily diet of any of the other villagers. Mother used to say, "If you want good beans, you must cook them in good water." So we children were sent down to the river, several hundred yards away, to fetch water for the beans. They were then cooked in the clay pot to give them a very special flavor. I have many pleasant memories of my childhood years. The days went by quickly, some filled with laughter and some with wranglings, childish pranks and adventures.

There were days of poverty, hard work and grief in our home, but none of these things caused our love for one another to diminish. In fact, they drew us closer together. We didn't have a big farm, so the children were sent to larger farms to work. It was especially difficult for us during the war years, 1914 to 1918. Father was called into military service and the following year brought us virtual starvation. During the winter of 1917-18, when I was ten years old, I was sent to work for the richest man in our village, "Grandpa" Kolyo. I received no wages, but in return for food I led the oxen while Grandpa, who was 87 but looked and acted much younger, ploughed his fields. Then in the summer I tended sheep on my uncle's farm nearby. The war ended and my father came home. This allowed me to resume my schooling. Even though we were very poor, my parents managed to send me to a little school in a nearby village. They were very proud of my ability to read and did all they could to continue my education. I began attending school dressed in patched, home-woven clothes and homemade moccasin-like shoes made of raw pigskin, with the pig bristles turned out. I looked a sight! When I got to the higher classes, I was ashamed that I did not have the regulation uniform and nice shoes. The result was that I shunned the company of other boys and kept mostly to myself.

I had my first pair of proper shoes when I was 17 years of age. When I put them on, my self-esteem grew enormously (probably too much!) and I began to look for friends among my classmates. I grew up as rather egotistical, and as an atheist. That's a bad combination! When I finished the town school I went to Ruse, a large city on the Danube River, to look for work. I knew only one person in Ruse, a former neighbor named Christo who had moved there several years earlier. Christo had a job at the water works and lived on the premises in a little room about six feet square. Although it was so small and most of the space was taken up by a bed, he agreed to let me share the room and we became close friends. This was in November, 1925. At that time there was much unemployment in Bulgaria and I couldn't find permanent work. I got an occasional job, but mostly lived off the salary of my friend, Christo.

One evening, Christo invited me to go with him to a nearby Baptist church, though he knew that I was a convinced atheist. Because of my friendship with him, it was impossible to turn him down. It was my first time in a Protestant church. I had known only of the Orthodox Church and thought that all churches were alike, so I was surprised to find that the interior of the Baptist church was quite different from the Orthodox Church. In fact, everything was different! The service was conducted in Bulgarian instead of the old Slavic language which the priests usually used and which few could understand anymore.

Instead of the monotonous singing of the Orthodox mass, I heard beautiful hymns sung to melodies of Bach, Mendelssohn, Beethoven and other great composers. Here the whole congregation took part; in the Orthodox churches, only the priests and the choir sang.

I even saw songbooks! Christo had already learned the songs and sang along while I followed the words in the songbook. The beautiful words, written to the praise of God, made a deep impression on me. I had never expected to hear an educated, intelligent pastor preach so gloriously of his faith in God, and in a language I could understand. In our neighborhood, there was no intelligent person who dared to acknowledge that he believed in God. "Religion" was for the old and feeble-minded in my opinion.

After the meeting we talked with two elderly ladies who were known in the city as having a good education. They talked to us about God and tried to prove to us that He existed, but despite what I had seen and heard in the church and all that the ladies had said, my proud intellect refused to acknowledge that there was a God.

For the first time, however, I began to wonder whether I was right.

That night a spiritual struggle began within me that lasted many days. The question was: Is there a God? In the Greek Orthodox Church of that time the priests didn't need to have any schooling and only old men and women attended the services. You never saw any educated people believing in God. At least, that was the way we atheists liked to think. We who had an education looked down on those "simple" men and women who claimed to have "religion" or believed in God. And now I heard educated and cultured people openly testifying that God exists! They told what Christ meant to them and had done for them. This impressed me more than all the sermons, and to this day, I am a strong believer in the effectiveness of "living testimonies" in bringing men to Christ.

I discussed my conflict with Christo and he said he would introduce me to a man who could help me. Shortly after, Christo invited a man to visit us. His name was Petroff. He read to us from his Bible. He was not an eloquent preacher but every word he uttered proved to me that God existed. He witnessed of how he knew of God's personal presence. When he told of what Christ meant to him, his face shone with the love of God. It was obvious to me at that moment that there was a God.

I saw Him in this godly man.

Petroff's testimony convinced me of God's existence and I began earnestly and intensively to seek God. I found I wasn't so much seeking God as God was seeking me. I received a wonderful life-changing experience of salvation in Jesus Christ, and Petroff became my spiritual father. Shortly afterward I went to live with Petroff to be closer to his Bible teaching and with his assistance got a job on the State railways. The work was heavy, but the joy of my new-found salvation in Jesus Christ made me buoyant with joy and peace. I was very happy in Christ!

Each night, Petroff and I would read from the Bible and talk together for hours about God's Word. In time others joined us until we had quite a little "flock" of believers. Gradually our little gathering took the form of a proper church and under the deeply spiritual ministry of Petroff we were greatly blessed by God. It was February, 1929, when Petroff said, "Haralan, God has His hand on you. He wants you for His work." I, too, had felt His hand upon me and leading me in this direction. I deeply loved my new found Christ, and prayed all night promising, "God, my entire life is yours. I am ready to give unto you all I have."

That promise was put to severe testing in the years ahead, but I never regretted it.

To serve Him is wonderful, but to suffer for Him is an even higher privilege.

To prepare myself for Christian service I attended Bible Institutes in Danzig and England, where I met a young Bible student from Sweden. Her name was Ruth. Like her Bible namesake, she was deeply dedicated to the Lord. She said, "Haralan, wherever you go, I go also." So I went back to Bulgaria not only with a knowledge of God's Word, but with a wife as well.

The years that followed were nothing less than a gift from God. A great time of spiritual harvest came to Bulgaria and in a few short years I was pastoring the largest church in the nation. At the same time, I evangelized across the land. God's hand was so abundantly upon all of us and the Word of God grew mightily in Bulgaria. For over 16 years I pastored my church and "doubled-up" as an evangelist in mountain towns and villages where the Word of God had not yet secured a foothold. The war years came and things were very difficult, but were only a little

19 ●

testing period for the great tribulation which lay just ahead of us.

In 1944, a dark menace came riding into our homeland on the heels of the Russian Army: the menace of communism. The communists slowly gained power while our country was lying prostrate at the feet of the Red Army.

At first the Communist Party was most cooperative with other political parties and even formed a coalition government. In three years, the other parties were banned, their leaders imprisoned and the Communist Party was in full control.

BULGARIA BECOMES "LITTLE RUSSIA"

We had heard of our fellow-Christians in Russia and what they had suffered, but little did we know that Bulgaria would become so like Russia it would be — and still is — called "Little Russia." We braced for the worst, but strangely the blow we expected did not come. In fact, a "twilight" period of religious freedom set in. It wasn't because the communists were *for* religious liberty. It was simply that they were *too busy* consolidating their political power and getting everything firmly in hand before turning to "deal" with us — as they put it. So instead of the blow we expected we suddenly had a great gift from God: three years — from 1944 to 1947 — during which God restrained their hand and allowed us to work.

And work we did! Day and night, month after month we evangelized, spread the Gospel and built up the faith of the believers before the dark night of communism fell upon us. As they had warned, we knew the communists would soon "deal" with us. Feverishly, with a sense of running out of time — we labored and God honored our labors with a great time of harvest across Bulgaria. I conducted several mass-baptisms in the Black Sea for the many young people who had found Christ. Undoubtedly, our feverish work for Christ during this three years "before the storm" caused us to be singled out for the "special" treatment which was to follow in communist prisons.

The *very intensity* of our work during the "calm before the storm" made us marked men. We didn't have long. As soon as the communists had consolidated their power we knew it would be our time.

BETTER SPIES THAN CHRISTIAN MARTYRS

The first sign that our time had come was a whispering campaign to slander the country's leading pastors. Despite this campaign, revival spread and new churches formed so the government devised a more subtle procedure. Gradually the pastors of the churches were taken away and replaced by persons who would be "willing tools" in the hands of the communists. They concentrated on putting their puppets into the pulpits.

Dedicated pastors soon found themselves displaced and could get only menial jobs such as streetsweeping. When puppet pastors had been put into many pulpits, the next target was chosen: the top Bulgarian church leaders from Baptist, Methodist, Congregational and Evangelical denominations. I was one of them.

A vicious slander campaign started. We were accused of being "spies." Better "spies" than Christian martyrs. We were described as "instruments of imperialism." At first when I heard this I laughed, asking Ruth, "Well, how do you like being married to an 'instrument of imperialism?' "

"So that's what you are!" Ruth laughingly replied.

The real truth meant nothing to those who were determined to destroy the Christian Church. We, the fifteen leaders of Bulgaria's Evangelical denominations, were publicly named.

It was obvious that we were not guilty of the charges laid against us, but a smear campaign was started to distort all that we had said and done in order to blacken us. It was noised about through the press and other media that we had betrayed our country to the English and the Americans. Thus began the campaign that was to lead us into prison and torture. During the following thirteen years and two months that I spent in prison I often wondered why God allowed such a thing to happen. The long period of self-examination helped me better to understand the Bible's teaching that we must go through suffering to enter the kingdom of God. Paul and Barnabas told the disciples in Asia Minor, "we must through much tribulation enter into the kingdom of God" (Acts 14:22). The Apostle Peter says the same thing (I Peter 1:6-7) "Wherein ye greatly rejoice, though now for a season, if need be, ye are in heaviness through manifold temptations: that the trial of your faith, being much more precious than of gold that perisheth, though it be tried with fire, might be found unto praise and honour and glory at the appearing of Jesus Christ."

Man's first natural reaction when looking at suffering is to think it is too hard to bear. We try to avoid it, but later we find that the suffering becomes of great value and is more precious than gold. Suffering was a fire which our churches had to undergo so that all that was hay and stubble would be burned up, leaving the pure gold shining more brightly than ever. In the process the "structure" of the church would be destroyed or subverted, but there would remain a true, living Church, the Body of Christ, the Underground Church.

This was all just ahead of us.

These were the events that had led me from being an ardent atheist to my position now as a pastor facing torture for Christ in the dreaded "White House."

THE CELL WALLS SPEAK

I was led down the corridor to cell number 21. The big key rattled in the lock and I was shoved in and once more was cut off from the outside world. In the cell was a young man named Tsonny. He told me he had been there for 3 months and was never given any reason for his imprisonment. In a corner of the cell was the bucket which for the next six months was our toilet. These buckets were a standard feature of prison life. They were emptied only rarely and sometimes overflowed. Often they took away the lid and the foul smell was overwhelming. There was only the bare cement floor on which to sleep and the walls were of grimy stone. They were cluttered with mottoes, prayers, slogans and quotations scratched into the surface with some hard object by previous occupants.

The walls were almost like a "diary" or chronicle of condemned men. In places the walls seemed to be painted dark red, but on closer examination I found the red wasn't paint. It was the blood of countless bedbugs which had been killed by former prisoners as the insects crawled up the wall. The "red walls" of other such cells were also to become common sights in the years ahead. That first night in the DS I killed 539 bedbugs, many after they had taken blood from me. To help take our minds off our situation Tsonny and I counted them. (We never tried that again!)

On the walls one could read about many of the afflictions and longings of former inmates. I could almost tell their personalities, their nightmares, their hopes, their dreams, reflected in these sad etchings. One etching read, "When you enter here believe in God and pray to Saint Theresa," evidently written by a Catholic. A Pushkin Elegy was written in Russian the full length of the wall. It contained three verses which I memorized. Above the door someone had scratched an old Latin proverb, "Dum spiro spero," which means "As long as I breathe, I hope." I felt I knew the former inhabitants of that cell by their scratchings on the wall.

What stories of human bravery, despair and crushed

dreams I saw on this cell wall and countless others during 13 years!

I made it a practice to scratch Bible verses and words of comfort on the walls of every cell I occupied, hoping those words would bring comfort and help to the next occupant. Cell walls were not only the "paper" on which I scratched Bible verses, but later were the "sounding board" for the "Prison Telegraph" on which I tapped the Word of God to the men in the adjacent cells.

How wonderful and just, I thought, that walls built to imprison men would become "paper" for the Word of God and the "wire" for the Prison Telegraph to send forth the Good News. But because this was the first time I had experienced such an ordeal, and because the first week had been such a shattering time, it was difficult for me to keep up my courage.

All prisoners will tell you that the first few months are always the worst. I said to myself, *If the man who scratched into the wall the words, "As long as I breathe, I hope," could keep hope alive, surely I as a believer can put my life entirely in the hands of God.* I gave myself a "lecture" and felt better. Even though I didn't know what the day would bring I had assurance, serenity and peace in my heart. Like Paul I was determined that "in whatever state I am, therewith to be content."

I spent exactly five months in cell number 21, from August 1 to December 31. Cell 21 in the DS "White House" became a "chamber of suffering" for me. Every time I think of it today the cold chills run up my spine. In 2 Corinthians 12:4, the Apostle Paul speaks about "unspeakable words, which it is not lawful for a man to utter." However, I should like to tell about the unspeakable suffering which is difficult to express with the human tongue or to put into writing.

Since I was exhausted from standing on my feet every night for a week, I lay on the bare floor and stretched out. All of a sudden there was a loud, cracking sound like automatic rifle fire coming down the corridor. "What was that?" I asked Tsonny. He smiled and explained that it had been done intentionally by the guards to scare the prisoners and prevent them from sleeping. The sound was caused by hitting sharply on the cell doors with an iron bar, making sounds like loud rifle shots. It was repeated every ten minutes throughout that night and every night for five months. It was almost impossible to sleep and that's exactly what was intended.

On the morning of August 2, I was taken from my cell to a comfortable office on the ground floor. To my great astonishment I found there a young man whom I knew very well. His name was Veltcho Tchankov. My heart leaped for joy when I saw Veltcho! I had known him since he was a boy.

I knew also that he was a communist. When the communists had come to Bulgaria on the heels of the Red Army in 1944, Veltcho had joined them immediately. In the three years since, he had become the Chief of the Secret Police in Burgas. Despite the differences in our ways of life, we had long seemed to hold a kind of mutual respect for each other. So I was glad to see him again and thought this was the first ray of hope since my arrest. But how Veltcho had changed! A month later I learned that Veltcho, my "old friend," was the one who had staged the whole campaign against all the evangelical pastors! I saw what power can do to a man.

The communists when out of power are often congenial, cooperative and mild. But let them gain power and you will see what they are really like! Let those who "play" with communism remember the lesson of Veltcho, the "kind" communist who gained power.

Communist parties out of power purposely seem "reasonable" and kind, but let them come to power and their true nature will be revealed. The prisons were full of men who thought the communists were just another political party. Many of the people who said they were "just another political party" and tolerated communists were executed when the communists took over. Let the Western countries who tolerate communist parties beware! Those "little" parties may seem mild now, but if they gain power, you will see their true nature just as we did!

I said, "Veltcho, it's so good to see you again." He looked at me with hostility and said, "We know each other, Popov, and I warn you if you want to see your wife again you must do exactly as I say."

"But what have I done, Veltcho?"

He shouted back, "Never call me Veltcho again. I am Comrade Tchankov and you are Prisoner Popov. Never forget that!"

He went on, "You must criticize your crimes. If you confess it will be much easier for you. The People's Government is very lenient and we will forgive all your crimes. We know you are a good person, but you must conform to us and the new society we are building."

These words, "conform to us," I heard the whole thirteen years.

Then a torrent of words poured forth from Veltcho's lips:

"I repeat, you must conform and confess your crimes!" he shouted. "If you refuse to obey me, you will be making the greatest mistake of your life and will live to regret it. You will learn we don't play around, and we aren't going to let you be a religious martyr. You would like that wouldn't you, Popov? Well, we're not going to give you that chance. If we made you a religious martyr it would only make the Christians stronger. We're not about to let that happen. Do you think we are stupid? We're going to slander and blacken you until even the Christians will say your name in disgust."

I was stunned by Veltcho's words. His plan was satanically clever and he spoke like an inspired man.

I replied, "The people of Bulgaria know me. They

will know the real reason." He only laughed. Only later did I realize I was up against specialists at making black look white, and truth look false.

The Nazis were cruel, but the communists were cruel and satanically clever. That is the only *real* difference between the Nazis and communists in practice. Veltcho's threats were later carried out with mathematical precision, point by point.

Veltcho ordered me back to my cell. I went in utter despair and told Tsonny about my conversation with Veltcho. He advised me never to confess to anything I hadn't done. The advice was good, but impossible to carry out during the following months.

I sat in my cell in semi-shock. I had thought the communists were just misguided men. But this encounter with Veltcho shook me deeply. I realized I was up against the cleverness and evil of *Satan himself*. For the first time the enormity of what I faced and the cunning of these satanically inspired men hit me.

THE "DEATH DIET"

It started with starvation. The feelings of starvation — like the feelings of love — are impossible to describe. My daily food ration was two slices of bread and six tablespoons of "soup" which was really flavored water, slimy and putrid. The diet was carefully and scientifically designed to barely sustain life — nothing more. The prisoners called it "the Death Diet." It consisted mainly of water and was enough only to maintain a weak pulse. At the same time, it was enough to stimulate the gastric juices, causing one to feel hunger more acutely than if he had nothing to eat at all.

If a person doesn't eat at all he gradually dies, but his taste buds are dormant and he is mercifully spared the hellish pangs of hunger. I wasn't spared. The two slices of bread and six tablespoons of "soup" came at 6 p.m. They were gone in two minutes and there was no more food until the next day at 6 p.m. The goal was to "break" me and I confess that starvation is a horrible and effective tool. The hunger made my body feel as if it had malarial fever. These feelings were with me day and night for the next five years.

It must be understood that the communists were not attempting to "brain-wash" me. They knew they could never accomplish this. Brain-washing means to completely and permanently change a person's mind and make his mind over to be totally dedicated to another and different way of thinking. The communists knew they could never do this with me and they didn't try.

They were out to *break my will* — bludgeoning, battering, torturing, abusing and starving me to the point where my will was totally broken and just collapsed. They knew that after my will was totally broken and they had what they wanted from me, I would regain my will and come back to myself. Thus, their tactic was not to brain-wash me, but to so batter and drive me beyond human endurance that temporarily I would simply lose my will. Brain-washing calls for alternating between good *and* bad treatment. Destroying a person's will is simpler — it requires only brutal, unrelenting beatings, starvation and torture building up to a rising peak and crescendo of horror where a person no longer has a will of his own. This was their tactic . . . and they began it with a fury and brutality.

Starvation, sleeplessness and standing with one's face toward the wall week after week are the chief "tools" in breaking a man's will. This treatment can transform an intelligent and rational person into an animal. The only thing that remains after such treatment is the animal's instinct to look for something to eat. My guard used to say that I "must become stiller than water and lower than grass."

On August 5, under the "death diet" I was put into solitary confinement and subjected to a 24-hour-a-day, non-stop interrogation. I had three interrogators, each one working an eight hour shift. This allowed them to keep up the physical and psychological torture 24 hours a day. This solitary confinement cell had one very unusual feature. The wall was shiny white, painted with a white high gloss enamel paint. I was ordered to stand facing the glaring white wall at a distance of eight inches and to keep my eyes open — wide open. My interrogator began to shout —

"You must not move one inch!"

"You must not close your eyes for one moment!"

"You must not shift your weight!"

"You must not move a muscle!"

"You must not . . . You must not . . ." on and on he ranted as I stood at the wall. After only a few moments my eyes burned like hot irons were in them. At 8 inches I was so close to the glaring white enamelled wall my eyes couldn't focus. I suggest that my readers try this for only a moment. One's eyes rebel. They fight to close or to focus and they can't. It is terribly painful and yet when I merely blinked, my interrogator struck me across the side of my face.

The pain in my eyes became unbearable. "Tell me about your spy activities!" shouted the interrogator.

"I am a pastor," I replied, "I have worked for Christ all my life. I have never spied." The interrogator gave me another blow to the side of my head. My ear rang from the impact of the blow and again he shouted, "Tell me how you spied for the Americans!"

Again, I replied, "I am a pastor, a servant of God. I have only worked for God. I don't know anything about your spy charges."

Later, as the years of brutality passed, I became hardened to such beatings and they affected me only physically. But then early in my imprisonment these blows affected me and disoriented me, psychologically as well as physically.

The interrogator who beat me was a big, grim man. In the years ahead, I had time to reflect on these guards and interrogators. I always tried to pray the most for a guard while he was beating me. I realized that in one sense they were sadder cases than those of us they beat.

What a tragedy was theirs!

Step by step, as they brutalized prisoners and beat us, they descended down the ladder of humanity to the level of beasts. Their faces, after a time, defied description and they became like animals.

We prisoners would eventually recover, but the guards suffered a permanent crippling of their humanity. Thus, during the beatings I tried to keep my perspective and prayed for them. I found that it actually eased the pain of the blows.

"Tell me about your spy work!" screamed the interrogator. "I am a pastor, I —" and before I could finish the sentence another ringing blow hit the side of my face. A pattern emerged during that first long day. I was forced to stand absolutely still, not moving a muscle, my eyes burning like balls of fire staring at the shiny white wall 8 inches in front of me. From behind me the voice of my interrogator would shout, "Tell us about your spy activities!" I would reply, "I am only a pastor. I have never done anything but preach the Gospel."

A ringing blow to my head followed, then several minutes of silence. Then again the question, again my reply and again the blow to my head. As the hours passed, the questions came less frequently and I wondered why the interrogator waited so long between questions. After an hour or two it dawned on me; time itself was their weapon. Time was on their side and they counted on its wearing effect to wear me down. Hour after hour that first day, the pattern of question, answer, blow, pause, question, answer, blow continued. I lost all track of time. I had only the terrible burning in my eyes and to close them for only a minute became an obsession with me. My body went numb. I lost all sense of time and was jarred into reality only by the different sound of the new interrogator's voice, signaling that 8 hours had passed and a new shift had begun.

Now the pauses between questions were longer, as long as an hour. They were in no hurry. The night came and passed like an eternity. Sleep weighted my eyelids, but even a brief closure would bring a blow. My legs ached. My whole body rebelled, yet I could not move a muscle. Everything became hazy and time itself seemed to cease.

Dazed, I suddenly heard the sharp, fresh voice of my first interrogator shouting, "So, Popov, you are still here! Well, I am rested. We shall start again!" Then it struck me. A full day had passed and the first of my three interrogators was back on duty again.

Hunger welled up in my stomach. I had been starved before, given only crumbs of bread, but now I didn't even have crumbs. When I had received them the crumbs had seemed so little. Now with nothing even the crumbs seemed like a feast!

The Fourth Day at the Wall

Hour after hour passed. Day after day came and went. The time from midnight to morning was the worst. I had now not slept, not eaten, not moved for four days. The interrogator watched especially carefully to catch me when my head nodded or my eyes closed. They took special delight in catching a twitching muscle or a blinking eye as an excuse for a blow. Also, they wore felt shoes so I couldn't tell whether they were just behind me or across the room.

On the fourth day my hunger left and deep thirst took over. The blood began to settle in my legs and they began to swell up. My lips were dry, cracked and bleeding. Then another dimension of punishment took place. The interrogators began to eat noisily and drink water close to me to increase my thirst. The torture was not only physical, but also very much mental.

The deep, burning thirst was like nothing I have ever experienced or heard about before. It was like a fiery ball of lava burning in my stomach and parching my lips.

A deep fever consumed and wracked my body. Dehydration set in and the agony became almost unbearable. To this day when I read of a man dying of thirst in the desert, the all-consuming pangs of thirst hit me again and wherever I am I must go and drink deeply of water.

Another enjoyed drinking water a few feet away from me and one twitch of my parched, cracked lips, and without warning I was hit.

The thirst raged on within me like a raging fever. To this day I can't explain how I stayed on my feet through those days and nights. It had to be God with me, for no man has the strength in himself.

Slowly, the questioning stopped. It became a waiting game, my interrogators waiting for my collapse. In my feverish condition, I began having hallucinations. Little spots on the white wall in front of me came alive. I saw faces of people, of Ruth and Paul and Rhoda, then of the guards. Swirling patterns of blazing color were like a mad kaleidoscope in front of me. I was certain I was going mad.

THE TENTH DAY

Still the collapse didn't come. I lost all track of time. One day blurred into another. My swollen legs became huge, engorged with blood from complete immobility. My lips were cracked wide open and bleeding. My beard was long, for I had not been allowed to wash nor shave since the day I was arrested. My eyes were balls of fire. Yet, somehow I stood. On the tenth night, sometime after midnight I heard my interrogator snoring as he dozed off. I moved my stiff neck to the right and left. Off to the left about six feet away there was a window. Since it was dark outside I could see a reflection in the window, like a mirror. I recoiled in horror. It was a *monster's reflection!* I saw a horrible emaciated figure, legs swollen, eyes like empty holes in the head, with a long beard covered with dried blood from cracked, bleeding and hideously swollen lips.

It was a grotesque, horrible figure. I was repulsed by it.

Suddenly, it struck me. That horrible, bleeding grotesque figure was *me!* That "monster" was me.

My numbed mind slowly absorbed this fact and tears came into my eyes. Suddenly, I felt crushed, so alone, so by myself. I felt as Christ must have when He cried, "My God, my God, why hast thou forsaken me?" I couldn't weep tears, but my body heaved with unwept tears. Then, in that moment of total, crushing hopelessness, I heard a voice as clear and distinct as any voice I have ever heard in my life. It said, "I will never leave you nor forsake you. . . ."

It was so audible I dared to glance to my dozing interrogator, certain he had heard it, too, but he slept on.

The presence of God filled the Punishment Cell and enveloped me in a divine warmth, infusing strength into the shell that was my body.

It had a definite, startling physical effect on me.

My interrogator awoke with a start. He came over next to me and could sense something had happened. He didn't know what, but he was so aware of the difference he rushed out and returned with another officer. They couldn't understand it. I heard the anxious, whispered voices of the interrogators behind me, trying to figure out what happened. I seemed to be so fresh and alive, infused with a new strength. I have never felt closer to God in my life than at that moment. He became so close to me, my heart longed to see Him. I had felt the presence of God so close and it was wonderful, superior to any feeling I have ever had. It was like a foretaste of what being with God in eternity will be like and I didn't want to go back.

I prayed for death. I longed for death. It was a welcome door by which I would see the Christ whom I had loved and served so long.

THE FOURTEENTH DAY

The presence of God buoyed me up for a long time, but on the fourteenth day the total starvation, thirst and burning fire in my eyes became too much. I was clearly dying. I felt detached. *So this is what it's like to die,* I thought.

Any minute I shall see Christ.

The guard saw that something was happening and rushed out, returning with a doctor. The doctor took one look at me and said to the officer, "This man is dying." Their voices seemed as though they came from a far distance. They evidently weren't ready for me to die yet, because I felt myself being moved. What must have been an hour later, I came to in my cell. From the look of horror on Tsonny's face, I must have looked hideous. I couldn't move. My legs were swollen up like an elephant's legs. My lips were cracked open and bleeding. My eyes were deep black holes in my head, the pupils flaming red. For a week I couldn't focus my eyes or use them properly.

As consciousness slowly returned, Tsonny told me the date. I couldn't believe it. I had been standing without food or water for 14 days! I cannot explain how it was possible. Later that day, they brought me food, water and let me rest. Painfully, my cellmate helped me lift my huge swollen legs high and propped them up against the wall so the blood would run down. I fell into a deep sleep. I thought the worst was over.

It wasn't.

The next night, after midnight, I was again called down for questioning, this time by an officer named Eleas. There were four or five others waiting for me in the room. As I stepped in I was met with jeering, scoffing and humiliation. Then they started hitting me. I swayed across the room and fell, was dragged up again and hit some more. Obviously they had decided to add more physical torture to the mental torture.

During all these things, I remained silent. Even though I had gained a little strength from my rest I was still very weak and the least shove would make me fall. They didn't hit me hard, for that would have knocked me unconscious. Finally, Eleas loaded his pistol, grabbed me by the collar, and half-dragged me out into the corridor. I was bleeding profusely from my nose. It was pitch dark. He pushed me ahead of him to the end of the corridor where there was a dim light burning. He kept his pistol pressed against my back all the time. When we reached the light he shouted, "Stop! Face the wall."

‘I turned to the usual position, noticing spattered blood and chips in the plaster from impacted bullets. Obviously, this remote, dark end of a subterranean corridor was where many others had met their deaths. Eleas turned off the light. It was cold and pitch dark. Death hung heavy in the dank air. Eleas pressed the pistol into the back of my neck.

"Popov," he said, "we've had enough of your stubbornness. This is your last night. You must die because of your stubbornness in refusing to confess your espionage. I am giving you your last and final chance. While I count to five you may think it over, and confess that you are a spy. If you are sensible you may live, but if you are not I will shoot you at the count of five."

I was sure he was going to shoot me, for thousands of others had been shot in the DS White House before me. I knew these people carried out their threats.

The thought of death as a bridge to eternity flashed across my mind. I would see Jesus! I was filled with certainty that this hellish torment would soon be over. It was as if eternity had already begun for me and only the formality of death remained. Mentally, I was prepared and was already "with Christ." I waited only for the shot to go off, and I would be taken up an angels' wings to Heaven — to Jesus, my Saviour. There was such a longing in my heart in that magnificent moment to see Jesus. How appealing this was for me. All this torture ended. To see Him! To be with Christ!

Many people don't like to think about death. They fear and tremble at the word "death" and see death as a forbidding black figure. *Why* do people fear death? First, because they don't believe in God. For those who have not accepted Christ as their Saviour death is the most terrible experience there is. People fear death because they are not sure of their salvation. Their sin makes them conscious that there is some accountability after death.

But for a person who believes in Jesus and is sure of his faith and salvation through the cleansing blood of Christ, there is no death. We do not believe in death, because there is no death for those who are in Christ Jesus. In John 11:26, Jesus said to Martha, the sister of the dead Lazarus, ". . . whosoever liveth and believeth in me shall never die." After that He asked her a remarkable question: "Believest thou this?"

If there is one certainty in this uncertain world it is the Word of God. Heaven and earth shall pass away, but the Word of God shall never pass away. Up to now, I had never imagined what death would be like, but for me death was not a dark spectre, but an angel come to liberate me. Death to me does not appear dark and grim. It is full of light and gladness, for Revelation 14:13 says, ". . . Blessed are the dead which die in the Lord from henceforth." And Psalm 116:15 tells us, "Precious in the sight of the Lord is the death of his saints." Truly, for those who are saved, death is not only a gateway to heaven but also a triumphal arch through which we march with victorious joy and a glorious song.

Eleas began to count slowly, pausing a long while between each number to give me a chance to blurt out my confession. "One . . ." a long pause, ". . . two . . ." another long pause, ". . . three . . ." he counted very slowly, all the while pressing the pistol to my head so I could feel it. He believed that I would be afraid of death. But Eleas couldn't see what was going on inside me! He didn't know that I was *waiting* for the moment when I would see my Master, whom I loved more than anything else, whom I had served and about whom I had preached.

When Eleas continued with a long, drawn-out f-o-u-r, something almost unbelievable happened. The Holy Spirit came upon me in a greater measure than ever before. It happened to me as it did to Gideon in Judges 6:34: "But the Spirit of the Lord came upon Gideon. . . ." I became as courageous as Gideon and as strong as Samson. I do not see myself as a courageous man. But Gideon's God is my God, and was with me in that dark corridor. Eleas paused after counting to "four." But he paused too long for me. I heard a voice coming from deep within me — fearless, strong, demanding. It shouted, *"Don't wait — Don't wait! Shoot me straight in the head!"* Eleas jumped back in panic and fear. He hadn't expected this, and neither had I!

He couldn't understand (nor could I) where my strength had come from! I had been so weak and exhausted that I could hardly walk. But Eleas was even more surprised than I was. I braced myself for the bullet, but instead I felt a cracking blow on the back of my head. In that fleeting moment before unconsciousness swept over me, I realized Eleas had intended only to bluff me into a confession, not to kill me. A pain of disappointment — so real it was physical — welled up in my heart, far greater than the pain splitting my head.

I was so deeply, deeply disappointed. I was ready to meet death, but I was still in this life. I was so ready to be with Christ, but I was still with Eleas. Why had death been denied me? Before unconsciousness swept over me, I cried out within my heart, "God, I was faithful to the death, but death didn't come."

I was taken back to my cell and thrown into it unconscious.

As I came to, Tsonny had pulled me over against the wall and was wiping the blood from the back of my head. To be so close to God, and to awaken back in the DS cell! It was a crushing disappointment, but I breathed a prayer, "Lord, not my will, but Thy will be done." I fell into a deep and long sleep.

Later, the cell door was opened and a new prisoner was let in. He sat in a corner of the cell as if he was ashamed and said not a word. Gradually, he became more talkative. He said his name was Nickolai Gantchef, that he had served for many years in the royal palace guard of our previous King Boris, and that he was now arrested on charges of being a monarchist and of taking part in some conspiracy or another.

Tsonny was suspicious of him, but I, in my naivete and still suffering from the beating, believed all he said was true. I later learned that this man had been placed in our cell to spy on Tsonny and me.

Shortly afterward, Tsonny was taken from the cell. A year later I met him again in another prison and he told me that Nickolai had gone to the leaders and said that Tsonny was wise to him and suspected him and they ought to remove Tsonny from the cell so he could get on with his job of helping break me.

Nickolai and I were left alone in the cell, and he picked up much information about me, which I, in my innocence, gave him. Later, I became aware of fellow prisoners who were forced to spy on their cellmates through threats of harm to their families. I later realized Nickolai's downcast look when we first met was from shame. But the Secret Police quickly learned a prisoner's most vulnerable points — his children, his wife, for example, and used it without mercy.

Nickolai's job was to find my vulnerable point. He quickly found it. It was, of course, my wife and children. I was worried sick about them. Ruth was all alone, with two babies to feed and care for, and here I was, powerless to help.

But even those informers I met in prison and who at times caused me much punishment, I tried to love and understand rather than hate. They, too, were victims like me. Pathetically, prisoners often tried to speak harshly about their own wives and children so the Secret Police would think they didn't care about their families, and thus would leave them unharmed and in peace.

Many times I have heard men curse their wives and children as though they didn't care — then turn, bury their faces in their hands and shake with weeping.

Informers were found not only in places where systematic campaigns were planned (such as the one against me); they were everywhere, in prisons, camps, homes, places of employment, and even in the congregations of churches. To improve their own situation in prisons and to lessen their own suffering, many prisoners made themselves available as informers. The communists cannot sleep calmly if they don't know about everyone — such as who thinks what about them, or who says what about them. Consequently, in all Bulgaria there was hardly a cell, a block, or a place of employment, or a church which didn't have an informer who reported what was said. It is just as bad today.

PREACHING THE GOSPEL TO THE SECRET POLICE

At the beginning of September, 1948, I was turned over to a lawyer named Peter Manoff, who was to conduct the interrogation until I "confessed." Every night I was ordered to write down information about myself, my work, friends, friends of friends — everything they wanted to know about me.

It seemed harmless and it would give me a chance to rest, so I started writing. I decided I would weave in a testimony of Christ in every possible place, with the slightest opening. They especially wanted me to write about everything that happened in my life. That suited me just fine. It gave me so many chances to tell my interrogators what Christ meant to me! I knew they had to read what I wrote, so I filled it all with the Word of God and my testimony.

Manoff was busy the whole day in court as a prosecutor and came in the evening to give me new assignments and appoint a new guard. The only sleep I was able to get during the whole month were short "cat naps." I was allowed to come back to the cell each morning, at noon and again in the evening, perhaps for fifteen minutes at a time. I received my ten ounces of bread and the flavored water they called "soup" every day.

I used this short time to rest and sleep a little.

I was extremely weak because of lack of sleep and undernourishment.

It would be interesting to read what I wrote during these nights. I must have written over 2,000 pages in all, often up to 40 pages in a single night!

Every night I was given a subject on which to write. It became a game with me to take the assigned subject and find a logical way to weave in a testimony about Christ. I really became quite good at this.

Whatever subject they gave me, I found a way of getting in a testimony! I don't think they appreciated it, but it was so carefully woven in, it seemed in place and a part of the whole. It infuriated them, but after all, Christ had been a part of my daily life since I was converted. And though they hated it, it was God's Word and they, of all people, needed God's Word.

One of the best chances came when they ordered me to write on my Bible training at Danzig — which teachers and friends I had there, what courses they taught. *That really was an opportunity!* I gave the lessons in detail, just as my instructors had taught me. I imagine these were the first communist interrogators to have Bible lessons! Then they asked about my Bible School days in London. I really plowed into that with relish. Here I was, in a communist prison, using communist paper and communist ink to tell communists the Word of God which I had been taught! They had said, "Popov, we want all the details!" And I gave them *all* the details! Those were some of the most wonderful days I had in prison. Telling about the Bible classes, brought it all fresh back to my mind.

One day, they said to me, "Popov, enough is enough. We don't want to know any more about your Bible School life and your fairy-tale God!" But, thank God by this time, they had been exposed to His Word, like it or not. They ordered me to stick to the situation in Bulgaria. Always, I tried to find a way to come right back to the Word of God and what the Lord meant to me. I really "stretched" some points, but I usually managed to get in my "Gospel message." I often wonder how many communists my message reached.

But they were smart also. The sheer volume of my writings enabled them to pick out isolated incidents here and there and twist them. Unknown to me, the persons mentioned in my manuscript were thoroughly questioned and harassed.

One of these persons was a Christian brother named Marko Kostoff who worked on the docks at Burgas, a port on the Black Sea. He was asked if we had talked together at the harbor, when we had talked, what we had talked about. In Bulgaria, a pastor usually calls on the members of his congregation in their homes at least once a month. During my visits I would talk about God, the needs of the family, and so on. If the husband worked in the fields, I would talk about the seed and the harvest. If someone worked for the railways, I would talk about what he did. In this manner during my pastoral visits to him I talked with Marko about the harbor and his work, as well as about spiritual things.

My interrogators decided to make political capital out of this. Marko recalled at his interrogation that we discussed his work at the harbor. He mentioned that we once talked about a barrel of cheese. They had been loading barrels labeled marmalade onto a ship bound for Russia and one of the barrels happened to fall to the dock and burst, revealing that it contained cheese. In Bulgaria at that time there was no cheese to be obtained anywhere because the authorities were secretly sending all supplies to Russia labelled "marmalade." Marko had told me about this strange-looking "marmalade." He recalled that we had talked about this incident.

In this way the authorities claimed that I "obtained information about activities at the harbor and passed it on to the English and Americans." Similarly, my church members who were railway and factory workers, recalled that they had talked to me about their jobs.

The authorities were carefully constructing a case against me, being most careful that I not appear as persecuted for my faith in God. One night I was led to a room on the fourth floor where I was ordered to sit and write. By this time, I was a starved skeleton moving in a stupor, a twilight world of semi-consciousness. The window opened into a courtyard, on the other side of which was a wing occupied by the Secret Police. I noticed a lighted window in a room over on the other wing. Through this window I saw a man being tortured. He was held down on the floor with his feet up in the air. Two men pinned him down while a third, armed with a hard rubber club, beat with all his might on the bare soles of the poor man's feet. I could hear the blows distinctly all the way through the closed windows and across the courtyard. The man screamed in agony and pain. The blows continued until the man became unconscious and still they didn't stop.

Surely that man never walked on those feet unaided again. The sight burned itself into me. Then, and countless nights to come, I closed my eyes so I couldn't see. I covered my ears so I couldn't hear. "O God," I prayed, "help me to turn off my brain and not think!"

Later, I resumed my slow painful writing, but my thoughts were with that man. I felt very sorry for him. Yet I was envious of him. I would have willingly traded places with him. His ordeal lasted only a few hours, but even if the torture lasted two days, it would be over for good then. He would be dead and his suffering over. I wished with all my heart that they might treat me like that, so that my suffering would end. I understood why they put wire nets over stairwells and bars on windows on high floors; these were not to prevent escapes but suicides. If you died, they wanted you to go *their* way, not by your own choosing. But my wish was not fulfilled. God's thoughts are not our thoughts, and the Lord had another plan for me. I didn't understand it, but I accepted it.

LEADING MITKO TO CHRIST

Nickolai left the cell at the end of October and I was left alone to rest — with the "Death Diet" continuing. Though I was hungry, I was now permitted to sleep, so some of my strength came back. I gave up fighting the bugs and other creatures that swarmed over my sleeping body. I needed the sleep more than I needed the blood they took from me. Most of my waking hours I spent in prayer. I wasn't so conscious of my hunger this way, and my spirit was uplifted.

Some days later, the cell door opened and a young man named Mitko, about 23, was brought into my cell. Poor Mitko was so young and frightened. He kept pacing the cell saying over and over, "I'm innocent. I'm innocent!" to no one in particular. How many times those walls stained dark red from crushed bugs must have heard this! He was pitiful. Every time a guard passed by he would begin to shout again, "I'm innocent!" He praised Lenin and communism loudly, hoping the guards would hear him talking like a "good communist" and let him out. It was a pathetic, desperate effort (I have often seen prisoners do this). My heart went out to him and I began to tell him of Christ and the hope we can have in salvation. For days I worked to penetrate Mitko's sheer panic and get through to him. One day the wild look left his eyes and he began to really listen. My heart rejoiced. I was really reaching him. Two days later, Mitko said, "Pastor, pray for me."

I knelt down with Mitko and together we prayed. He prayed so earnestly and intensely, so from the heart, that the cell floor where he knelt was wet with tears. He had a wonderful and true experience with Christ. He became peaceful, quiet, with a deep inner satisfaction from God. Then I knew if nothing ever came of my imprisonment except this one soul led to Christ, it would be worth it all.

One day the cell door opened and a guard came in. He had a paper to say that Mitko was to be freed. Mitko could not believe it but the guard showed him his release papers. The guard left to return for Mitko a little later. While waiting to leave Mitko told me,

"Pastor, here in this cell I have found God because of you, and I shall follow Him all the days of my life." The guard returned and Mitko clasped me farewell. I have never again seen him but I am sure Mitko stayed true to Christ.

I was alone for ten days. I felt so close with God in solitary confinement that I spent the time in praise and worship. Such close communion with God! I talked with Him. He comforted me. It was a spiritual feast for me. During this time, I received new strength, though my body was wasted away to nothing. Tears of joy ran down my face. Here, in the DS prison, alone and with nothing, I had everything — Christ. Stripped of everything, without any worldly distractions, I found a deep and beautiful communion with God. Joy and peace flooded my soul. My body ached with starvation but my spirit has never been closer to God. Lying starved, alone and too weak to move, I felt I could reach out to God and be taken into His arms.

I was freer in that cell than I ever was on the outside. Free from the world and all its pressures and pursuits, I found a closeness to God such as never before in my busy days. Prison stripped away the cumbersome distractions of life and I found a spiritual depth and unity with Christ. Prison either destroys a man from within, or it gives him a deep spiritual strength. Prison, where one is cut off from life, often brings to light man's most genuine and deep resources. Strangely, being in the worst of conditions has often brought out the best, the most sacrificial in men.

In the years to follow, I saw prisoners care for one another as closest brothers. Friendships were forged in common suffering. I have often witnessed a starving man in prison take his only daily ration of bread crumbs and give them to another prisoner weaker than he.

God's presence surrounded me and strengthened me. It filled me. I will never forget those ten days. Early on the morning of the tenth day, I looked out of my cell window toward the factory across the street. To my astonishment, I saw the clear form of a cross on the rooftop of the factory! I think probably the shadow of two big chimneys was formed by the sun lighting the chimneys in such a way as to cause a cross. But, to me, it was a sign from God. I stood at the cell window a long time, looking at the cross and thinking of the cross on which Jesus died and of His love and goodness. Suddenly, a voice as real as any I have ever heard said, "My son, this is your cross which you must bear. Prepare yourself for more suffering."

Though I knew something terrible was about to happen, the sign of that cross gave me a feeling of confidence in God and, looking through the bars on the cell window, I started singing a favorite hymn.

> Beneath the cross of Jesus
> I fain would take my stand.
> The shadow of a mighty rock,
> Within a weary land:
> A home within the wilderness,
> A rest upon the way,
> From the burning of the noontide heat,
> And the burden of the day.

With tears running down my cheeks I sang on,

> I take O cross, thy shadow
> For my abiding place:
> I ask no other sunshine than
> The sunshine of His face;
> Content to let the world go by,
> To know no gain nor loss,
> My sinful self my only shame,
> My glory all the cross.

I sang this song to the end, and my heart was filled with sweetness. Tears poured down my face. They were not bitter tears, but as we Christians in Bulgaria say, "sweet tears."

As I finished the song, the door opened and I was led downstairs for another period of torture. My ten days of quiet communion with God were over. My biggest ordeal was now here, with my "show trial" coming up.

THE SHOWDOWN COMES

My "show trial" was already scheduled, dates set and I had not yet been broken. The officers were now becoming desperate. They had to break my will within a few days or else. It was eight o'clock when I was led back down the staircase with the wire netting, and again to the office of Comrade Manoff, the chief interrogator. Though I walked as if carried away by the effects of the great blessing I had received, I was very weak in my body. My legs almost gave way beneath me as I walked. The accumulated effect of what I had been through had taken its toll. God's Word had been accomplished in me: the body was weak, but the spirit was strong.

I greeted Manoff politely, but he turned his head without responding. There was another person in the room whom I had never seen before. With a fierce shout he commanded me to face the wall, so I placed myself once again in this familiar position. It started all over again. Manoff had three interrogators to assist him. I could tell this was the showdown. Their voices were fierce with hatred. They had evidently been reprimanded for failing to break me and this time, they were not going to fail. The oldest was the one who had ordered me to face the wall. His name was Dimitri Avrahamoff. The other two young men looked to be only in their early twenties. The younger of the two was a young man whose eyes were filled with consuming hatred. His face was physically contorted with hatred toward me. How young, but already how reduced to animal-like hatred and frenzy!

How this man needed Christ! I thought.

The three rotated every eight hours, while I stood facing the wall again — without any sleep, keeping my eyes open, just as I had done the fourteen days earlier. Yet, then I had some reserve of strength. Now I had none. The "Death Diet" had taken its toll.

After twelve o'clock the first night, the young man so filled with hatred came on duty. He watched my every move, noting if I shifted my feet to rest a little, or if I didn't stand at attention. He scoffed and jeered at me. As I have already mentioned, the hours after midnight are the most difficult for a prisoner, for that is when the body demands sleep and one has to fight to keep awake. No matter how much one tries to keep awake, he dozes, even if he is standing, and falls. When this would happen to me, the young man would silently steal up behind me and hit me with a stinging blow to the side of my head that left my ears ringing.

Immediately, following the blow, he kicked me in my shins with his heavy boots with all his might. Once, after I had fallen, I was commanded to hold my arms straight up. After about ten minutes they became so tired they fell down. With a loud curse he screamed for me to raise my arms again, but I didn't have the strength to carry out his order. Another blow. Another kick. He then ordered me to lean against the wall on two fingers, which is still worse. These men know every painful contortion the human body can be put into. The last hours of the night were indescribably painful. It was still only the first night, but at least I had succeeded in holding out.

With the new day came renewed strength. It is interesting to note that one doesn't feel as tired during the day as he does during the night. I learned much about the human body and its endurance during these times.

The torture, beatings and vicious kicks continued during the second, third, and fourth day. The side of my head was swollen. My shins were in constant pain from the kicking. I became weaker, receiving neither food nor water. Again my hunger vanished and instead, there was the thirst I had experienced before. The blood had again left my head and gone to my legs, which had swollen to twice their normal size. My face had shriveled, my beard had grown quite long, my lips were cracked, blood ran down my beard again. I was experiencing what had happened once before, but it was more painful this time.

One day blurred into another. I passed out and often collapsed. They revived me with a bucket of water and stood me up again, raining blows and curses on me. I felt nothing but fire, fire, burning fire from thirst and pain. Then God's Word came to me in a flash! "But all these things will they do unto you for my name's sake . . ." (John 15:21). "For unto you it is given in the behalf of Christ, not only to believe on him, but also to suffer for his sake" (Philippians 1:29). For His sake! For Christ's sake! This glorious thought renewed my strength. My spirit began to talk with God. The most difficult hours — the ones after midnight — came and went and I didn't even know where the night had gone. Soon it was the morning of the seventh day.

Manoff, the interrogation leader, came in again and wasn't at all happy to see me looking so refreshed. It was now the seventh day and he was waiting to see me break. The trial was only a short time off and they were getting desperate. He called out an order to Dimitri, who seized me from behind the shoulders and shook me savagely. I felt the Spirit of the Lord filling me again. Dimitri swung me around, clenched his fist, then something happened to me.

I can't explain it to this day. At that moment every muscle in my body became as hard as stone. The weakness of a few moments before entirely disappeared. The effects of six days and nights of starvation, standing, and blows, the cursing and the three months of torture and starvation were forgotten in a moment. My weakened, shrivelled body straightened out. I came to my full height before Dimitri, straight as a statue. Dimitri towered over me, for he was a big, strong man. His first three blows landed squarely between my eyes. My nose swelled and blood gushed forth, but I felt no pain. My muscles were hard and my body rigid. I neither swayed nor fell from weakness.

More blows followed but incredibly I felt no pain, the front of my shirt was covered with blood. Dimitri hit me cruelly. My face was a mass of pouring blood, open cuts and swelling. But still I felt no pain! Instead, I felt a surging power come over me and I held my face up to present Dimitri with a better target. I moved toward Dimitri and he started backing up. I followed him. My face was near him again. I cried out, "Hit me! Then you will understand. Hit me! Hit me!" Shaken and pale, Dimitri slowly turned and collapsed heavily in a chair.

I had followed him across the room demanding that he hit me, propelled by a force not my own. Now I stood over him as he slumped in the chair. Suddenly, the supernatural strength I had felt drained from me. I felt so weak I couldn't stand. I collapsed and crumbled to the floor like a wet rag. The incredible experience was over. I lay there as the room was filled with silence and bewildered interrogators. Finally, they hauled me up and shoved me against the wall. I leaned against it weakly. I stood there all night.

The next day was November 7, the day I lost my will. I remember falling as if someone had hit me over the head with an iron bar. I began to have hallucinations. The room was filled with snakes. They crawled on the floor, up the walls and furniture, and came straight at me and slithered over all my body. The knot-holes in the wall became faces — mad faces laughing hysterically at me. I was on the verge of madness. The snakes, the faces — all seemed to be swirling around and around and I felt myself sinking down, down, ever down. I had sunk to the edge of madness. Through months of beatings, starvation and torture, I had fought the good fight.

I had stood more than a human body was meant to stand. I came to the end of myself. "O God," I cried. My will was broken at last. They had won this time.

Under the influence of this psychological treatment and physical torture a person is transformed into something like a phonograph record, which speaks and sings whatever has been cut on it. They fed us the words and like a machine we repeated them. If they told me I had killed my own mother I would have mechanically repeated, "Yes, I killed my mother."

I was no longer human, but a human tape recorder. I had been battered, beaten, brutalized, starved, until I was a human robot. I was ready to confess anything. Having reduced me to dough, Dimitri began to knead me as he desired. He seemed quite a specialist in this field. It wasn't the first time he had succeeded in bending a prisoner to his will. He said to me, "You are a spy of the first class."

"Yes," I replied.

"That's what I like about you. You are on the right track. Sit down. We will wait until Manoff comes, then you can go to your cell and rest." I sat down on a chair. My head swam with dizziness. From that moment, I believed and knew that I was a spy. That is how all fifteen of us church leaders became "spies."

In the morning, Manoff came. He grinned from ear to ear at the news. I was taken to my cell, given food, and left alone to rest. I lay for a long time while my body and nervous system quieted down, then I slipped into a deep sleep.

An elaborate series of "confessions" was prepared by the communists for me to sign. I signed them. If they had ordered me to sign that God was dead I would have signed. My own will had gone so far it would simply go no further. On December 31, at 4 p.m., I was told to get my belongings together. I had a mattress and blanket which I had received from home after my will was broken, and I rolled them together with my clothes and a few other things. Two guards led me out to a car waiting outside. The day was bitterly cold. On Sofia's streets, the trees and telephone poles were covered with a thick layer of frost. They looked so beautiful. We drove down a number of streets, then found ourselves at the back doors of Sofia's Central Prison.

The D.S. had finished their work. I had left the "White House."

They had "prepared" me for the trial.

THE WOODEN SHOE SONG

"But before all these, they shall lay their hands on you, and persecute you, delivering you up to the synagogues, and into prisons, being brought before kings and rulers for my name's sake. And it shall turn to you for a testimony" (Luke 21:12, 13). With these words, Jesus prepared His disciples for what was going to come. During the whole history of Christianity these words have been fulfilled over and over and it still happens in our day. The Bulgarian evangelical congregations experienced it to an especially great degree.

The "prison" in my case was a five-story building surrounded by a big yard. Around the yard was a fifteen-foot-high and three-foot-thick stone wall. In each of the four corners of this fortress was a high tower in which a guard was always on duty. The Central Prison is similar in construction to all the other prisons in Bulgaria, but is larger than any other. Built many years before the communists came to power, it had more than 350 one-man cells, each containing a bed, a table and a chair. Since the floor was made of cement, the prisoners had to wear wooden shoes. In this prison, built to accommodate 300 to 400 prisoners, there were now over 5,000! One whole section of the prison had been taken over to accommodate the pastors and the witnesses, numbering 170 persons in all. After the trial, some were freed, others sent to another prison, and still others were sent to concentration camps.

My cell was at the end of a corridor, next to a toilet. The toilet was where the prisoners brought their buckets and dumped them. My cell was like a cold storage plant, rather than a place for a person to live. The floor was littered with rubbish. I placed my straw mattress and blanket on the cement floor and lay down on them. It was a cold day, and though I wore every item of my clothing and wrapped myself in my blanket, I could not sleep for the cold.

It was New Year's Eve and I paced the cell, wrapped in my blanket, listening to the clacking of the prisoners' wooden shoes on the cement floors. We called it the "Wooden Shoe Song." It was caused by thousands of prisoners pacing back and forth trying to get warm. During the thirteen years of my imprisonment I had only one pair of leather shoes, but I can't begin to count how many pairs of wooden shoes I wore out. Tonight, I was hearing the wooden shoe song for the first time. I would hear its eerie sound many times over.

Chilled to the bone on this dreadfully cold night, I and the other 5,000 prisoners watched the New Year come in.

Later, Ruth told about her first visit to me. She said, "Early in January, a prison guard came to me and explained that I together with the children could visit my husband in the prison. I hadn't seen my husband since he had been arrested on July 24.

"At the prison, we were greeted by the superintendent who was very friendly. Then we were taken to a waiting room, and Haralan was led in by two guards. There we greeted each other, while an official sat nearby to listen to our conversation. My husband's legs, arms — his whole body — were swollen to twice their normal size. I asked him if he had been sick, since he was so enlarged. He glanced around nervously and put his fingers to his lips, so I knew I wasn't allowed to ask him. He then said aloud, 'My clothes are a little tight. If you could send me some larger pants, it would be good.' The ten minutes of our visiting time were soon up — it went much too fast. Then Haralan was led out again."

Seeing Ruth for the first time since my arrest, I asked her, "You see what you got into marrying me. Perhaps it would have been better for you to have remained in Sweden. I have brought you only suffering."

Tears came into her eyes and she said, "No, my place is with you."

After her visit I received good food to "fatten me up" back to my original weight and medical attention to repair the physical damage. I must not show any signs of what I had been through. For six months I had not been allowed to wash my face or body or shave. You can imagine what I looked like!

BROKEN, BUT NOT BOWED

The courthouse in Sofia is the largest single building in Bulgaria. How appropriate that it is so large, it gets much use. It takes up a whole block in the central part of the city. My trial took place in the most beautiful and important courtroom in the courthouse — Courtroom 11.

Microphones and movie cameras were installed on both sides of the auditorium so that the proceedings could be filmed. Journalists from foreign countries were among the special guests, among them, *The London Telegraph, The New York Times* and other great newspapers. This was to be a history-making trial in which I and the other fourteen highest church leaders of Bulgaria were to be tried at the same time. Also present was the "Red Dean" of Canterbury, H. Johnson, who was flown in especially for the trial.

Our relatives were given a special admittance card. The hall, which held over 500 people, was packed. One by one we were brought up from our basement cells with a policeman on either side of us. We went to our seats without any form of communication with one another. Nevertheless, we couldn't help staring at one another when we saw the "well-attired" pastors, each dressed in his own neat, well-pressed suit. What a contrast to the filthy prison rags we had worn for six months!

How did this happen? Two weeks before the hearing began, we were told to write to our families and request our dress shirts and well-pressed suits. They also were permitted to send us as much food as they were able. Besides this, we had been getting nourishing and fattening food from the prison kitchen for the previous two weeks. All of this was to insure there would be no trace of the suffering we had been through, since we were to appear before the foreign press and diplomatic officials. We were to look well-fed, well-clothed and well-treated — communist deceit at work!

The court consisted of three judges, but they were only puppets. The real decisions were in the hands of the DS people sitting in the first row of the audience. The script had already been written well in advance. The charges were read by Bulgaria's Chief Prosecuting Attorney who was assisted by State's Attorney Tsakoff.

The first one on the stand was the Baptist pastor, Nickola Michailoff. His hearing lasted six hours. He was the most transformed and the one most ready to say what the communists wanted him to say. Actually, Pastor Ziapkoff, who was the leader of all the evangelical congregations in Bulgaria, should have been the first to take the stand, but evidently the DS didn't quite trust him to humble himself.

Pastor Michailoff proved to be an "important witness" against all the pastors, especially against Pastor Ziapkoff.

His testimony alone would have been sufficient to condemn us all to death, but because we had "confessed" we were "reprieved" to serve prison terms, the intention being to show communist "mercy."

The second on the stand was the Methodist leader, Pastor Janko Ivanoff. He repeated what the Baptist pastor had said and confirmed his testimony in every respect.

The next day the newspapers were filled with the terrible "confessions" of espionage by the pastors who had "sold" Bulgaria to the English and Americans. According to the papers, "the people" demanded the most severe penalties. It was evident that everything in the newspapers came from the DS. In fact, we later learned the articles had been written weeks before! Early in the morning we were given copies of the papers, so we would realize that our situation was hopeless and there was nothing else for us to do but to confess, repent and plead for clemency. Our confessions were written out like sermons and we were told that, after we had read the confessions, we were to begin moaning and crying in "repentance."

Only my brother, Ladin, had not yet been broken. He had even refused to wear a necktie into court as a token of his resistance. That night the British Broadcasting Company in London broadcast that Ladin Popov was the only one of the fifteen pastors charged with espionage who refused to confess. They (the BBC) proclaimed him the hero of the trial and he truly was. Ladin is physically very powerful and has been able to withstand much of the torture. Being unmarried, he did not have a wife or children to be concerned about. This helped him mentally.

The trial was a tragic "black" comedy, written, produced and directed by the DS. We pastors had been beaten and starved until we were like tape recorders. Before the trial, we had been deprived of the two most important factors in a human being's life — his will and his reason. In reality, we were only tape recordings played by the DS people — recordings which played back their will, wishes, thoughts, and lies.

Tape recordings reproduce only what has been recorded on them.

According to communist teaching, the end justifies the means. This allows communists to use lies, deliberate deception, murder, and every measure possible to reach their goal.

In our case, they had specific objectives.

First, the case against the nation's leading pastors was designed to destroy the evangelical churches. Secondly, it was to destroy the faithful pastors in one blow, so "puppet" pastors could replace us. But, it was really Christ and His teachings which were being judged when we pastors were placed on the witness stand. Once more, the devil had false witnesses and had found false accusations to get rid of Christ, the Light of the World. He was tried before Pilate who took his orders from Rome, mocked, sentenced to death, crucified and laid in a sealed tomb. We were following in His footsteps.

But regardless of how shrewd, clever and wicked the devil was, he didn't succeed. The reason is found in Paul's words to Timothy: "The word of God is not bound" (2 Timothy 2:9). God's Word cannot be destroyed. Sooner or later, truth will be victorious. Just when the devil thought he was victorious, Christ arose from the tomb. A lie is always a lie. Neither Marxists nor Leninists will ever succeed in building an earthly paradise upon a lie.

The witnesses for the prosecution were like the chief priests who saw to it that Jesus would be sentenced to death. The allegations made against us had no basis in fact, yet the empty words and fabricated circumstances were repeated time after time.

An engineer who worked in a marmalade factory testified that he had discussed with Pastor Ivanoff how the marmalade was "vacuum packed." Later, the engineer found some money in a book of his. The prosecuting attorney asked him, "How do you think it got there? Don't you believe that Pastor Ivanoff put it there as payment for the information he got from you?" After some mumbling, the witness said, "It is clear that he must have done it."

Such were the testimonies against us! The witnesses didn't tell the truth. Their perjury, however, was involuntary. They said what they were forced to say and I felt no ill will toward them.

The testimony continued for eight days; the whole trial lasted twelve. It was engineered like a puppet. The strings were pulled and the puppets moved. After the hearing of evidence the prosecuting attorney made a speech which lasted for four hours, which contained more politics than accusations. He described the international situation and said that "international imperialism" tried to keep the workers from fighting for their ideals. He said that through us, the pastors, the imperialists were trying to demolish communism.

When he had finished, his assistant delivered a tirade of damnations, vilifying each of us personally. During the entire hearing, both the prosecution and the defense pointed out how wicked the crime was and called for the death penalty for what they charged was espionage in politics, economic affairs and matters of national defense. Neither the prosecution nor the defense could give an example of anything we had done to deserve such severe punishment. Our lawyers, who were earning big money every day for "defending" us, supported the prosecuting attorney's propaganda and condemned us.

Only two of the defense attorneys dared to tell the truth. One of them was not a communist; he was there because he was one of the ablest and best-known lawyers in Sofia. In his defense statement he said, "Your honor, these pastors have been prosecuted as spies. Isn't it our duty to find out what their espionage consists of?"

He continued: "Pastor Mishkoff had sketched a map showing a road from Plovdiv to Pestera. According to the prosecution, this map was passed on to the

Americans. Are the Americans so simple that they could not go to the nearest book shop and buy a map of Bulgaria which shows not only all the roads in the country but also the railroads? Such maps are sold openly."

The prosecuting attorney leaped to his feet as if stung by a bee. He bellowed, "Mr. Toumparoff, you have no right to say that! Don't you know that today everything is secret in Bulgaria?"

Toumparoff immediately realized the seriousness of the prosecutor's tone, and the implied threat so he changed his tactics and adopted the same compliance used by the other attorneys on both sides.

Pastor Vasil Ziapkoff, the leader of the evangelical congregations, received the worst treatment. Despite his innocence of the charges laid against him, his lawyers advised him to confess, repent and ask for mercy, otherwise it would be impossible to escape the death penalty.

When he testified on his own behalf, this man we knew as a firm and solid servant of the Lord, cried profusely. He, too, had passed through unspeakable sufferings. Everyone looked at Pastor Ziapkoff in surprise. But it wasn't Pastor Ziapkoff who spoke, it was a "tape recording" that played back the song which had been composed by the DS. Even the tone and sound of his voice wasn't his. After the court hearing, we didn't see Pastor Ziapkoff for three years. His torture had pushed him over the brink of insanity and it was three full years before he recovered. Under the circumstances, timidity and fear gripped the churches — the second plan of the DS was beginning to work.

One after another the leading Christian laymen were called before the DS and sharply told they must renounce their acquaintanceship and fellowship with their former pastors. The newspapers began printing notices from members or leading Christians in the different congregations saying, "I express my disgust for

the pastors' activities and renounce my acquaintanceship with them."

As in Elijah's day a remnant refused to bow down
to Baal, and so there were those in the congregations
who stood by us. There were pastors who did not
write renunciations in the papers. However, one by
one, these pastors were soon ostracized and forced to
leave the ministry. Some were even sent to concentration camps. Others pushed brooms as street sweep-
ers in the very cities in which they had pastored.
Many of these faithful, ostracized pastors began "underground" meetings in homes at great risk.

Soon communism came into the Church itself in the
form of the "New Pastors" appointed by the DS. Some
of the young people and the more active members
were sent for at night by the DS. They were beaten
viciously during the night in a way which left no
marks. In the morning, they were released and forced
to promise to tell no one what had happened — not
even their wives.

One young Christian was summoned to the DS
every night for six months for nightly beatings. By
various means they tried to get him to promise to tell
everything that happened in the congregation. He refused. His wife noticed these nightly absences and
saw him return white and shaking from his all-night
beating sessions. He never told her of his sufferings.

The same methods were used on many other young
Christians throughout the country. Fervent Christians
and active members were especially sought after by
the DS. Many were not able to hold out, and bowed
to the will of the authorities perhaps in order to remain in the congregation. Fear of being reported determined one's conduct. In many cases, one knew
who the informer was, but one never dared to say it
openly because the DS could reach anyone they
wanted. I am reminded of the prediction in the Bible
that man will be betrayed by his own relatives.

Many Christians in other countries can never understand how shrewd and wicked are the powers of darkness. This is because they have never sat alone in a prison cell, completely helpless and hopeless. No matter how many books are written about it, only those who have experienced the ways and means that were used can ever comprehend what Satan can devise to torture men.

On March 8, our sentences were announced. The heaviest sentences fell on the leaders of the various denominations — Pastor Vasil Ziapkoff, the religious representative of United Evangelical Churches, Pastor Janko Ivanoff, Assistant Representative of the United Evangelical Churches, Pastor Georgi Cherneff, Assistant Chairman of the United Evangelical Churches, Nickola Michailoff, Chairman of the United Evangelical Churches. Each was sentenced to life imprisonment and confiscation of all his property by the State. Their families were left with nothing but the clothes on their backs.

The other pastors and I, members of the Supreme Council of the United Evangelical Churches, were sentenced to fifteen years imprisonment.

Pastors Jontso Drenoff, Zakari Raicheff and Ivan Angeloff were each sentenced to ten years imprisonment.

Pastor Mitko Matteff received six years and eight months imprisonment; Ladin, my brother, was given five years imprisonment. (He had never broken so they found another trumped-up charge for him.) Pastor Angel Dinoff and Pastor Alexander Georgieff were both released on probation. Angel Dinoff was immediately selected by the communists to be the president of the Evangelical Congregations. During the whole time of his arrest, it seemed that he was being prepared by the DS for this task.

The communists knew an outward attack on the churches would unite and strengthen the believers, as it has done down through Christian history. So they decided to destroy or control it from within. The communists had found him a very willing instrument. It was quite evident that he was a faithful supporter. To this day the communist tactic is to close some churches and install their own men in those that remain open.

THE TRAGIC SUFFERING OF OUR FAMILIES

After the trial, we were returned to the prison, to disappear from public view. But now it was our families as well as ourselves who suffered. Persecution came not only from the enemies of the cross, but also from the newly-installed "pastors," including Angel Dinoff. The people were warned that anyone trying to assist the arrested pastors or their destitute families would be sent to a concentration camp.

One of the pastors from northern Bulgaria collected a little money which he sent to Ruth and Pastor Cherneff's wife. He was accosted in the street, grabbed by the collar and asked savagely, "Who gave you permission to collect money for the arrested pastors' families?" The old brother lifted his hand toward heaven and said, "God."

Once Ruth was down to her last penny. Paul and Rhoda were crying from hunger. She fell to her knees and prayed, "God, we have no food. We have no money. Haralan is in prison. God, I am at the end of myself. Help us."

A little later that very day a letter arrived from the above-mentioned old brother, enclosing a postal money order for enough to pull her through the emergency!

Later Ruth, Paul and Rhoda were ordered out of the house we lived in. This intense suffering of families of Christian prisoners was carefully planned to increase the agony of the men imprisoned.

Ruth was concerned that her family in Sweden know the truth about our trial. Due to the poor postal services, we hadn't received a letter from them for some time and didn't know whether her letters had reached them. Then one day she was consoled in an unexpected way. An ordinary postcard arrived from a relative. It read, "We have heard, we have read, and we understand the whole thing."

The fear of the communists went so far that the New Pastors requested their members to find out who had dared help Ruth and my children. The family of Pastor Cherneff had been forced to move to Svistov, a little town near the Danube. One day, Mrs. Cherneff was in Sofia on an errand and in the evening she went to a meeting in the church where her husband had served for twenty years. Although it was raining hard, and everyone knew Mrs. Cherneff well, the informers were present so no one could invite her to stay overnight. So Mrs. Cherneff walked the streets all night.

At first, Ruth had a job. It was ironic. She was to clean Angel Dinoff's church every other day. She also received a small monthly salary for playing the organ at services. It wasn't long though before Dinoff was warned by the authorities that in this way he was helping the imprisoned pastors' families, so he made it clear to my wife that she was no longer needed.

Then a sister in the congregation, who was sick, asked my wife to take her place at work. This was how my wife found a job as a night cleaning woman. She kept that job for a whole year before her employers found out she was Haralan Popov's wife. She was immediately dismissed.

Ruth struggled every day to keep our children fed. It was a lonely, desperate struggle to stay alive. Later, I learned that even our Christian brothers in the free world did nothing to help us. It is a shame on the conscience of the Christians of the free world that thousands of Christian families are suffering like this now — alone and unaided — in communist lands.

Ruth had not a penny of support. She and the children survived on a few carrots slipped to them by a courageous Christian who defied the New Pastors' warnings. It was a dangerous, precarious existence for Ruth and the children. The communists always cause the families of imprisoned Christians to suffer at least as much as the prisoners themselves. This is to increase the mental suffering and burden of the prisoners.

One cannot describe the agony of a father or husband locked helplessly behind bars knowing his wife and children are at that moment almost starving, driven from town to town like rootless animals. It is a burden far worse than starvation for a man to bear.

I have seen strong men who could take almost any physical beating go mad knowing what their wives and children were suffering — and being unable to help.

This is the tragedy of our fellow Christians who are imprisoned in communist lands today.

"You're a Dead Man, Haralan Popov!"

After we had been sentenced, we were sent back to the Central Prison and put in small cells. For a time the food and conditions were improved. In the cell with me were Pastors Cherneff, Angeloff, and Matteff. Ladin, my brother, was also with us for a short time but he was quickly transferred elsewhere. This was the first time we had all been together since our arrests, and we began talking about what had happened and what we had been through. We were now slowly coming out of this state of being semi-robots and human tape recorders, and were regaining our senses.

As we did, I said to the pastors with me, "We have faced not men, but Satan himself. Though he has done his work well, I for one am more determined than ever that in the end God will triumph. Brethren remember, 'He that is in you is greater than he that is in the world.' They have won the battle, but with God's help we will win the war."

Pastor Angeloff replied, "Haralan, that is true. If God be for us, who can be against us?"

At once we noticed that Pastor Matteff acted strangely. He approved the communists' handling of the affair and took exception to our claims of innocence. Our conversations with Matteff were guarded and we came to realize that the DS had placed him with us to act as an informer. Several times, he was called away to be interviewed by the prison superintendent. Tragically, he had not only been broken physically, as we had, but his inner spirit had collapsed and he had become an eager tool in their hands. Prison either broke a man inside, or it strengthened his resolve. It was so sad to see Pastor Matteff crumble. My heart went out to him and I prayed for him earnestly. The satanic power had done its work well.

I was taken to a little office where one of the cruelest members of the DS, Comrade Aneff, was waiting for me. Standing beside him was a man I had not seen before. He was dark and thin, with extremely fierce eyes and the features of a drunkard. Almost immediately, he jumped on me and began to beat me all over my body. I fell under the rain of blows, while on the floor he kicked me with all his might and screamed horrible obscenities. He screamed, "Popov, we know you! You've been trying to start a plot with the other pastors. We're going to teach you who will triumph over whom!" He ordered me taken to the dampest, deepest cell in the prison. As I was led out he screamed, "You're going to rot down there by yourself! You'll never see the light of day again! You're a dead man, Haralan Popov!"

Pastor Matteff had done his informer's work well.

Two guards led me down to the basement floor of the prison. It was a good 50 feet below the surface. They roughly pushed me past the cells and on down an unused corridor. There, at the end, was a heavy metal door, rusty from the dampness. As I was pushed through it I saw another flight of stairs going almost straight down like a ladder. I descended the steep steps into the cold dark dampness. The only light now was from the guards' flashlights. I felt as though I were descending into the very pits of hell itself. I waited at the bottom of the steps as the guards made their way down the steep stairs. It was inhumanly cold with an unearthly blackness, blacker than I have ever seen before.

The guards took me by each arm, led me down a narrow walkway to a cell door. Opening it, they roughly shoved me in and locked it. I heard their footsteps leave, going back up the stairs to the world above.

It was deathly quiet and totally black. I couldn't see my hand in front of my face. I felt around like a blind man, found the tin drinking cup and tapped on the walls, but I got no reply from either side of my cell. I was all alone down here in the black bowels of the earth. Then the enraged communist's words struck me, "You'll never see the light of day again. . . . You're going to rot down there!"

I resigned myself to being forgotten down here in this deep, forgotten crevice far below even the lowest level, left to rot. And it wouldn't be long before a man would rot here. I felt the walls and they were wet with moisture dripping down. Deep in this forgotten cell so unbelievably dark, I got on my knees and prayed, "God I know there is no cell deep enough, no iron bars strong enough to separate me from You. God, be with me. Give me strength."

The floor of the cell was so wet from subterranean underground moisture I couldn't lie down. I felt my way around, over to the corner and huddled down there with my arms wrapped around me for warmth and went to sleep. I don't know when I awoke. In such absolute darkness one loses all track of time. It is like being suspended in another world. I tried to measure time in my mind, but it began playing tricks on me. Without some usual references, stars, daylight, shadows — something — a man loses all sense of measuring time. Even the blind have braille clocks, or other means. Imprisoned in that absolute vacuum of black space I had nothing.

For the first time in over a year I began to fear for my sanity. Had I been here for a day? or 20 days? For an hour, or for a week?

Only occasionally would I hear a voice, an iron grate would open and a metal plate be scooted on the floor with a little water and three or four carrots or a rotten potato with worms in it.

I now resigned myself to spending the rest of my life here. Mentally, I had accepted it. One day while I was praying, the hopelessness of my situation struck me full force. Starved, beaten, forgotten here, I knew there was no hope of ever getting out. It was a high-ranking officer who told me I would "rot" here and he meant business. Tears came to my eyes. For weeks I had been like this. "Oh, God," I cried.

Then something happened which has never happened before or since. A light glow began to shine and a warming sensation filled the cell and enveloped my weakened, starved frame. I felt strong arms around me, cradling me in the arms of Christ Himself. That same voice which I had heard when I had stood at the wall for two weeks spoke again. I can never describe that voice. Overwrought with love and compassion, Christ spoke to me saying, "My son, I shall never forsake you. My arms are around you and in them I shall comfort you and give you strength."

Tears flowed down my cheeks as I was held in the embrace of Christ. I know some readers may think this extreme, but when I was at the point of madness and despair, Christ let me know He had not forgotten me there huddled in the blackness of a forgotten cell in the bowels of the earth. It was a beautiful loving embrace and a moment that made all the suffering worthwhile. How I love Him! If all men in the world could only know this Christ in His beauty and love!

Now I was with Christ and content to wait for death to be with Him. He talked with me, comforted me and His presence filled the cell in an almost physical way. He held my hand in His nail-pierced hand. He knew suffering and shared the suffering of His children.

Those were precious, precious days. I communed with Christ as, getting weaker and weaker, I waited for death.

Then at some time much later, I heard noises of footsteps and men talking. My cell door was flung open and a brilliant flashlight shone in my face. "Popov, get out of there! You're coming with us!" a voice shouted. I could hardly move from having stayed in one position for so long. They half carried me and half dragged me out, pushing me up the stairs. When I saw even the dim light of the basement cells, my eyes rebelled against the brightness, being accustomed to total darkness.

Finally, I was back in the cell block where I had been before. Thrown in a cell, I asked the prisoner inside what the date was. I had been down there for 35 days and would never have gotten out, but the officer who ordered me there "to rot" had been transferred. Evidently God still had a purpose for me in this life.

Later, in the corridor, I met a little hunched-over man. He was Pastor Ivan Angeloff, who had gone through the same treatment as I. Pastor Angeloff and I were taken to the eighth department of the prison and put in an empty cell. We found some boards with which to make beds so that at least we no longer had to sleep on the cement floor. The very first night, the inevitable bedbugs were waiting for us. Attacking in swarms, they fell from the ceiling like raindrops. They swarmed over everything, especially us. Evidently we were the first prisoners in this cell in a long while, and the bugs had missed their meals.

We could never sleep under such circumstances, so we spent the night pacing the cell, killing bedbugs. We got a little sleep during the day when the bedbugs were not active. At night we took turns sleeping. While Pastor Angeloff slept, I stood "sentry" duty killing the bugs and keeping them off him. When I slept, he did the same. By the third night, the number of bedbugs had been considerably reduced, but the walls of the cell were decorated with red spots, which soon turned black.

In the middle of June we were moved to a large three-cornered cell which contained twenty other pastors — some from another trial which took place after ours. Our trial was only the start of the war to wipe out support of the churches. Now, for the first time, we were allowed a short walk outside every day. It was great to breathe fresh air again and see the blue sky and sunshine. I felt like a new man, even though I was still surrounded by prison walls. One day, I noticed a tiny, green blade of grass growing through a crack in the cement. As our guard looked elsewhere, I quickly bent down and picked it. You can't imagine what that tiny blade of grass meant to me. It was green and living. It was the first contact I had had with the outside for nearly a year. To hold that little blade of God's grass caused my spirits to soar.

Some days later, the superintendent of the prison visited our cell. He looked cheerful and informed us that we all would be given work to do — but first we had to become members of the "Cultural Society" in the prison.

The Cultural Society was a circle started by the Secret Police — the DS. In every prison, the DS set out to indoctrinate the prisoners. Actually, the Society was designed to "brainwash" us and to supply the DS with information about all the prisoners. The only thing that concerned them was the attitude of each prisoner toward the regime. The prisoners were also "trained" in the circle. At the end of the training, they were graded either "intractable" or "reformed."

CLASSIFIED AS UNREFORMED

The Cultural Society developed into a strong organization with reports, choral songs, theatre performances and courses (for example, on Marxism, Leninism, the cultivation of vineyards or agriculture). The most important courses were on communism. No matter what the course, the lecturers always managed to bring in a good deal about communism's two main figures, Marx and Lenin. Capitalism was condemned: it was intolerable and must be annihilated. Communism, however, was the greatest and most humane political system there was! Of course, all of this was so crazy and untrue that the lecturer himself didn't believe it. His bored, listless and empty words made him like a record player. The same words, the same sentences, the same expressions, the same reports were repeated over and over. It was sickening, but we had to endure it.

In the beginning, we didn't realize the purpose of the Cultural Society. When we did realize its objectives, there was no way to escape it.

Let me point out again the difference between breaking our will and "brainwashing" us. My will was broken after six months of being beaten into helplessness, until my human body reached its very limits and physically crumbled. It was temporary.

Brainwashing is "permanently" convincing someone communism is good. They could break my will, but they could never "brainwash" me! During the time they tried to "convert" and brainwash me, I was given work as a book-printer and type-setter. The other pastors worked in a cardboard factory.

Within two months, the prison authorities realized that I could not be "brainwashed" and gave up on me. I had "failed the course" and was marked for a hard-labor prison.

On December 1, my turn came. I was working in the printing shop when I was told to pack my things and take them to the auditorium. I had a mattress, a blanket, two quilts, a pillow, a suitcase containing my underwear, and a basket of food. They gave us plenty during their attempts to brainwash us. That was the only good thing about the "brainwashing" period!

In the auditorium, I found thirty other prisoners waiting further orders. Evidently, we had been given up as hopeless. Now the rough treatment would start again, as it was before our trial. In the evening, a covered truck arrived and we were ordered to get in, with our luggage. There was no window in the back of the truck so we had no idea where we were going. When the truck stopped we found ourselves at the Sofia railway station. We were locked in a small room which was cramped with the thirty of us, but we sat on the floor and tried to sleep.

Next morning we were put on a train for our new destination, Sliven. There are two prisons in Sliven, the "old prison" in the city proper and the "new prison," where we were taken, half a mile from the station. The prison was a large, five-story building which originally had been a macaroni factory. It was surrounded by a fifteen-foot-high wall, with a watchtower at each corner. It was dark when we arrived. We were taken to Department Eight which, as in all prisons, is the worst.

Because the building was not originally a prison, the cells were a little larger than the one-man cells at Sofia's Central Prison. Ours measured fifteen by six feet, but there were fifteen of us in it, and a place had to be found for the ever-present bucket, so it was more cramped than anywhere else we had been.

We were packed in like sardines in a can. The first thing we did was to measure the walls, then we marked off a sleeping space a foot wide for each man. Among the prisoners was a famous Bulgarian poet, Trifon Konieff. He was a wonderful, jovial man. We all liked him very much. Trifon was so big that he could not possibly sleep in a foot-wide space, so each of us gave up one inch of his space, so that Trifon could have a little extra. We carefully measured it off. This gave us a space exactly eleven inches wide. Because there was no floor space for our luggage, our bags and boxes were hung up on nails driven into the walls. All the other cells were the same.

At night, we all slept on the same side. If anyone wanted to turn over, we all had to turn at the same time, in unison. During the day, we sat in our little spaces. This enforced idleness gave me a wonderful opportunity to talk to the men about God. They were almost all eager to know more.

The only window in the cell was in the ceiling. Even though it was always open, the air was hot and stuffy. It was summer and the cell was packed with sweating, perspiring men in one hundred degree heat. We wore only undershorts, and still the perspiration poured from us. The only relief was our half-hour walk in the prison yard once a day.

It was awful to have to return to the humid, stuffy cell after our brief respite outside, but no one resisted. I never learned if the Sliven prison was a "discipline" prison, but the treatment was much tougher than in the other prisons. Now that I had been labelled "unreformed," the other prisoners and I were back on the "Death Diet." We received only the scanty ten ounces of bread, plus soup which tasted even worse than the other soup we had had. It was like eating black oil. The fish soup was full of floating fish eyes. But, I ate it, eyes and all.

NIGHT SOUNDS

There is nothing more frightening than prison insomnia. In the stillness of the searing hot night, one could hear the sounds of the prison.

There was the uneven breathing of the prisoners

packed up against one another. It was easy to tell which men were having prison nightmares through the uneven breathing. Who could know what crushed dreams were theirs?

There was the measured creak of the corridor floor caused by the guards' felt shoes as they walked back and forth. From time to time a padlock ground open and there were footsteps and whispers. Someone was being taken for interrogation or a beating.

As I lay awake pressed in my eleven inch space on a floor full of sleeping bodies, my mind often went to Ruth, Paul and little Rhoda. Where were they? What had happened to them? Ruth's worn, haggard face that time we met before the trial haunted me. Were they hungry even now as I lay here? Did they have a shelter over their heads? Worst of all, I could do nothing to help them. I had been separated from them nearly two years and it seemed like an eternity. Thirteen more years of separation loomed ahead!

"O God," I prayed in the stillness of the sleepless night, "what will happen to them? Keep them, protect them, help them." These nights filled with prison insomnia were the worst. Over and over, I would close my eyes and not see. I would cover my ears and not hear, but I couldn't turn off my mind.

Someone in a nearby cell, packed as tightly as ours, would groan. What were his nightmares, fears and destroyed dreams? Stifling hot and smelling of the bucket and the sweat of unwashed bodies, its silence threaded with the groans and cries of sleeping men, the air was heavy with despair. One could only hear the sounds of men who had lost all and whose hopes were that the night would never end, for sleep offered the only escape from reality.

In Sliven, and in the years to come, the nights were always the worst. Nighttime was a favorite time for the beatings and torture. The worst hours were from eleven to 3 a.m. One whole floor of one wing was given over to interrogation at night and no doubt equipped with the latest "interrogation equipment."

Over the screams of the tortured came the shouts and curses of the torturers. Often, I tried putting cotton in my ears to drown out the horrible cacophony of distant screams. The nights were when men had time to think, to remember what might have been. It was at night that many men went mad. I could hear their ravings as the mind snapped, refusing to work any longer, and the guards would come and take them away. Those were the sounds of a prison at night.

I especially tried to help men through these trying nights, and helping them helped me.

Soon time came for the DS to classify us. Class One consisted of political prisoners, pastors, priests and such. Class Two, the criminals, murderers, rapists. Then, each class was divided into three categories. The very worst "criminals" were Class One, Category One. That's where I was put. We were singled out for the worst of treatment. Each year we were classified. To be transferred to a better class, one had to be more inclined toward the new regime. During the whole of my prison term, I was kept in Class One, Category One. Evidently they gave up on reforming me, but it still seemed strange being officially labelled more dangerous than a multiple-murderer.

But I could see the communists' point. My faith and witness *were* more dangerous to them. They are not ignorant men. They recognize faith in God is their worst enemy. For 13 years I had to sit through lectures on Marxism and communism. I never "graduated," but stayed in the same class. I left prison an illiterate on this subject. It seems I just couldn't learn how one builds a communist society.

There was a large group of men who just gave up, and agreed with everything. They were not only transferred to a better class, but were released from prison much earlier than the others. They had been "reformed" and were considered "trained."

Sometime afterward, a large group of political and religious prisoners in Sliven, myself among them, was ordered to pack. Altogether we were about two hundred and eighty persons. We were taken to the station and put into three freight cars, while our baggage was put in an open truck.

We were taken to the nearest railway junction and we wondered in which direction we would be heading. On the open car which carried our luggage stood a brakeman, whom I recognized as an old acquaintance. Surreptitiously, I signalled to him, asking him if he knew where we were to be taken. He replied by marking the frost on a window pane with the letter "k." Then I knew that we were on our way to Kolarovgrad.

Kolarovgrad Prison had just been built and in some places, it was not quite finished. They had not only one-man cells, but two-man cells also. The windows were larger than usual, and there were boards on the floors. We were told that this prison was intended for political prisoners who were discipline problems, and that the treatment would be particularly severe, so we were expecting brutality. But the officials turned out to be more humane than those at Sliven. They must have ignored their orders and ruled the prison themselves.

We were located in the north wing. Our cells were clean and well ventilated, and everything was completely new. The only bedbugs were those that came in with our luggage. (Which were plenty!) Our cell was made to hold twelve persons and there were only eight in it, so for the first time since being imprisoned we had a good place. Our food ration still consisted of half a loaf of bread daily, but the soup was simply delicious. Though we could never say we were full, we didn't have the hunger pangs we had in Sliven.

Some of my fellow-prisoners had been high ranking officers. One of them had attended an American school in Sofia and could speak English very well. Others could speak it a little, so all the prisoners in our cell began learning English. I ministered to them as their "prison Pastor." I taught them a beautiful hymn which we all sang in English. It goes:

What a fellowship, what a joy divine,
Leaning on the everlasting arms;
What a blessedness, what a peace is mine,
Leaning on the everlasting arms.
Leaning, leaning,
Safe and secure from all alarms;
Leaning, leaning,
Leaning on the everlasting arms.

After a year of horror in Sofia and Sliven, the stay for us there was a beautiful testimony to the wonderful grace of the Lord. It was like a new life, though I knew it would be short-lived.

During October, we were allowed to see our loved ones for the first and only time that year. Ruth came with our little son Paul, who was just at the age when children are minus their front teeth. I noticed immediately that Ruth had lost a lot of weight. She told me she was at that time working as a charwoman for the newspaper *Trud* ("Work"). To my surprise, through the double iron grating between us, I was allowed to hold little Paul in my arms. Their visit was a tonic to me.

A GIFT FROM GOD

Shortly after this visit, I received all my underclothes and shirts through the mail. I was greatly disturbed. When this happens, it usually means that a man's wife had died. It struck horror to all prisoners, when it happened to them. I wasn't allowed to write or receive more than one letter every three months, so I wasn't able to find out the conditions at home. For three months I never knew from one moment to the next if Ruth were dead. I was in terrible torment. If Ruth were dead, what about Paul and Rhoda? My fellow prisoners tried to console me and convince me that there was some other reason, but my despair grew greater. The thought that there was no one to take care of my children, who were still very young, nearly drove me out of my mind.

I prayed for grace and left the matter with Him. The next morning, carrying the bucket to the toilet, a fellow prisoner named Dragan came up to me. He whispered, "Haralan, your wife and children have gone to Sweden." Dragan worked in the prison office and was in a position to learn of things outside the prison, but he had run a big risk in telling me news of happenings outside. He would not tell me more than that bare piece of information and it took me some time to find out the whole story.

It seems that the cashier in the office, who was not a communist, knew the pastor in Kolarovgrad. The pastor told the cashier that Ruth and the children had managed to get safely to Sweden and asked him to pass on the news to me. The cashier was not allowed any contact with the prisoners, so he passed the message to Dragan whose work allowed him occasional contact with us. Several days after Dragan had told me the news, I received a letter from Sweden from my twelve-year-old daughter, which said, "With God's help we have come to Sweden and are now in Stockholm."

I had never known such ecstatic joy in my life! My wife and children were delivered — saved from further persecution and poverty. The long hand of the DS couldn't reach them in Sweden. The heavy burden which depresses and kills many prisoners — the cares and troubles of their families — had fallen from my shoulders. How I thanked God! The whole cell-block rejoiced with me! Even non-Christian prisoners were caught up in my joy of all joys and said, "Thank God" with me. They shared my happiness. I knew I would almost certainly never see my loved ones again, but at least they were safe.

I cannot begin to convey what this meant to me. The remaining years in prison were easier to endure. I was no longer afraid of the communists. They had me, but they could not touch my family! Ruth, Paul and Rhoda were free. With this great, crushing load off my shoulders, I determined to enlarge my ministry as prison pastor. What could they do to me? My wife and children were free. They could torture me, but they couldn't touch my one really vulnerable spot — my wife and children! Much suffering and torture lay ahead because of my witness for Christ in prison, but no longer was I a prisoner. Surely, there were walls and bars around me, but no one could take away the inner freedom inside me.

Later, I learned it was the intervention of the Swedish government on my wife's behalf that secured her freedom. She was a Swedish subject married to a Bulgarian. Only this saved Ruth and the children.

This news was the turning point for me. It was the greatest gift God could have given me. The last restraint, the fear of bringing suffering to Ruth and the children, was lifted from me. Now I would teach, preach, witness and work for Christ in every prison they put me in. They had lost their hold on me. They had a "different" Haralan Popov now!

Shortly after this wonderful news, I along with four hundred other prisoners were ordered to Persin, an island prison in the Danube river, for hard-labor work. We were pushed into box cars so crowded that we had to stand the whole trip. In the evening, we started on our way to Belene, the railraod station nearest the island. The officer in charge was so afraid of our possible escape that he insisted on closing *even the air vents* of the freight cars at night! We covered about fifty miles during the night and were then shunted into a siding where we stayed until late afternoon.

The day was very hot — over one hundred degrees inside the crowded box car. Men panicked and beat on the sides of the box car begging for air, for water, but no one would help us. Men began collapsing from heat and thirst. We were packed so tightly, when a man collapsed, he couldn't fall to the floor. There was no room. He remained upright, though unconscious. The heat must have risen in the afternoon to well over one hundred ten degrees, all in an airless box car.

Finally, as a result of our yelling and knocking, the officer allowed the doors to be opened a crack to allow our water bottles to be passed out for filling. We covered a further thirty miles during the night. The next day, it was the same story. We sat on a rail siding from 7 a.m. to 5 p.m. in horrible heat, thirst and exhaustion — always standing.

At the end of the second day we were parked in a siding only six miles from Belene. In the heat more of the prisoners lost consciousness. When this happened, the officer finally allowed the doors to be opened and the unconscious men were carried out and laid on the grass. After they had been given artificial respiration, they regained consciousness. This incident caused the officer to allow the doors to be left open a few inches, and when the sun went down, our journey continued. It was dark when we arrived at Belene station, and we found armed soldiers everywhere. We took our baggage and then marched across the fields to the river, escorted by the soldiers. Bent under the weight of our baggage, we could barely hold out, but anyone who fell soon scrambled to his feet again to avoid being trampled by those marching behind.

Wet with perspiration, we finally reached the prison's administration building which was surrounded with barbed wire, and marched in.

PERSIN — AN ISLAND OF HORROR

"I . . . was in the isle that is called Patmos, for the word of God, and for the testimony of Jesus Christ" (Revelation 1:9).

Belene is a village of eight thousand people situated on the Danube River which forms the northern border between Bulgaria and Romania. The prison administration building lay right on the banks of the river. Many of the personnel lived there. Four hundred yards off-shore lies the island of Persin, pear-shaped and about six miles long and two or three miles wide. The main island is flanked by two smaller islands: Sturez, measuring about four hundred yards across at its widest point accommodated a women's prison camp; Berzina, the other island, was the smallest of the three.

The western part of Persin and the coastline on the north and south were higher than the center part, which contained several lakes. The highest part of the island was in the east.

The whole colony was divided into five different barracks. Ours was about a mile from the administration building. The prison barracks were low huts made of willow branches braided together and daubed with a thick layer of clay. The roofs were made of dried sunflower stalks and straw. Each barracks housed five to seven hundred prisoners, and all but one were built on the ground. The other was on a "plateau" two or three yards high.

About four and one half miles away on a hill at the eastern end of the island was Barracks Number Two. Number Three was between the first two and had barns and a farmyard. The prisoners who were trusted by the authorities tended the cows and sheep there.

Barracks Number Four was the women's camp on the island of Sturez. It was on high ground and well built. In the summer of 1952, about one hundred and fifty women lived there and took care of the pigs. The fifth barracks was in the village of Belene and was for the criminal prisoners.

It was dark when we arrived at the administration building and climbed onto big rafts which were towed to the prison island behind a motor boat. During the following summer a pontoon bridge was built, which speeded up transport between the mainland and the prison island.

When we reached the prison island, our spirits lifted. For the first time, we had no guards behind us, no revolvers at our heads. I drank in the fresh night air and lifted my eyes to the starlit heavens. My thoughts went back to the days when I was free. It seemed like another world. When I reached the barracks I lay down on the floor and slept.

Our first day on the island was spent getting settled. We saw that there were towers placed a mile apart all over the island, where guards were stationed. A one-hundred yard strip along the coast was forbidden territory and anyone found there was immediately shot.

We soon learned Persin was a camp of extreme hard labor. Of the six thousand prisoners there, only *a few hundred survived*. The next day we were divided into forced-labor battalions. It was harvest time and those who had come before us had already cut the forage crop. Our task was to harvest and thresh it. Each of us had to harvest eight hundred square yards a day, though few of us had ever done any threshing before in our lives. The first day I was exhausted. I worked fifteen hours straight but still couldn't fulfill the quota. After returning to our barracks at nine o'clock we had to stand at attention while the foreman lectured us for not completing the work. The lecture lasted two hours more. Late that night we finally got to sleep, only to be awakened again at 3 a.m. to begin another day's work. We worked from

3 a.m. to 9 p.m. — 18 hours a day. Every muscle in my body ached.

In the marshland, masses of mosquitoes hatched during the summer. They descended on us in dark clouds and stung us like wasps. The prison leaders were displeased because we were not completing the production schedule and ordered our food ration to be reduced. This started a vicious cycle. Our reduced food rations weakened us more and caused us to harvest less. Then, in punishment, our rations were cut still again. Many died all around me through overwork and too little food. It was a desperate struggle to work — or less food. Less food meant less work still, and in turn, even less food. Then death. We shared our food with the dying, but many died anyway. Guards moved among us in the field beating any who were not working fast enough.

One night, two prisoners escaped and made it across the border to the free world. Several days later, two more escaped, but they were caught near the border of Greece and brought back. The bravery of these four made it harder for the rest of the prisoners. The guards were cruel and never needed to answer to the authorities if someone was shot. To frighten the prisoners and prevent them from escaping, they often simply killed a prisoner at random. We never knew who would be next. Just on impulse, a guard would single out a prisoner working in our midst, walk over to him, put his rifle to his head and pull the trigger. This happened several times close to me and once to a dear friend of mine.

Once, a guard was walking toward me and had his rifle pointed at my head and was actually squeezing the trigger when another guard called his name, distracting him. He walked off and didn't return.

When we finished the threshing, several weeks behind schedule, they put us to digging the field. Each prisoner was ordered to dig up 1,120 square yards of weeds a day. With a plough we could have possibly done it, but it was impossible for us to meet our quota of 1,120 square yards of weeds with a hand-held hoe. The heat of late July dried out the ground and water holes with the result that drinking water became scarce. The heat beat down on us unmercifully.

After we had finished with the corn, we began in the sunflower fields. The field we worked was three or four miles from the barracks and each morning and evening we marched the distance with guards on both sides of us. Since the whole work schedule of the island was behind due to the poor condition of the prisoners, the prison director became alarmed and ordered a speed-up of the work. Instead of marching to the field, we were ordered to run three to four miles with guards on horseback chasing us and cracking long leather whips on our backs. We staggered into the fields almost too exhausted to move. In the evening we were chased back to the barracks by the guards on horseback. They took great joy in beating the half-dead, staggering line of prisoners. And woe betide any man who fell. The guards set upon him with a fury of lashing until ribbons of flesh dangled from his back, face and arms.

This continued until the sunflower crop was harvested. It was a very expensive crop in terms of human suffering! Again, it shows the low value put on life when men look upon mankind as only "matter," with no soul. One day during our work among the sunflowers, a little rabbit came hopping by. We were starved and like skeletons, we thought only of one thing: to pull up a blade of grass to eat. And here comes a rabbit! The prisoners all surrounded him and one killed it and hid it to take back to the barracks at night. We were eating the "Death Diet" and also working.

In the evening three guards rode up to our work area and ordered the one who had killed the rabbit to confess. No one did. When the guard realized that no one was going to confess, he ordered us back to the barracks at a fast run. By the time we managed to get through the lashings and reach the barracks, an informer must have told the foreman who had killed the rabbit, for the unfortunate man was called forth. He was about 55 years of age and very thin.

They started beating him savagely with a thick club. I have seen — and been the victim of — terrible beatings, but this poor man was beaten so horribly I couldn't stand to look at him or listen to his screams. His screaming was horrifying, piercing, almost incredible. It filled all space. Compared to his, the cries of a woman in labor were a cheerful sound.

He was beaten until one of his eyes dangled out of his head. I have never seen such cruel and meaningless treatment in my life. The prison guards continued beating the old man on the head, groin, arms, legs and back until he was unconscious. We could do nothing but stand there and try to contain our feelings. Some prisoners wept with rage and frustration. All this because a starving man tried to get extra food.

Again, I remind my readers, when man is without God there is no limit to his depravity or to the depths to which he will sink. These guards descended the ladder of humanity step by step until they had no humanity or kindness left. I fought to contain my anger at seeing this brutal beating. I told myself the sick guards were to be pitied, but I confess this was one time I had to struggle to control my feelings.

SECRET MESSAGE IN A PHOTO

By the middle of September, I felt I just couldn't stand it any longer. I was weak after the hot summer and heavy work. I had not received a letter or food parcel from my loved ones for about four months.

I thought something bad must have happened に them.

One evening, I was told a letter had arrived for me. It was from Sweden and came just at the right time to strengthen me. There were several pictures of my wife and children, as well as a picture of the front of the church in London where Ruth and I had been married in 1937. My wife and children had been there since and had taken the picture. Across the front of the church could be read the words, "Prayer changes things." I realized this sign had been photographed to assure me that there were friends praying for me. It was Ruth's message to me. The censors who went through all mail for just such words as those hadn't noticed it on the church photograph!

Ruth was very shrewd getting such messages to me. I was more grateful to God for this letter than I would have been for a food parcel, even though I was starving. Too often these words, "Prayer changes things," are repeated mechanically, but they had great meaning to me — there on that island of horror. Every day I saw how the Lord's hand protected me, so when I received Ruth's letter, my spirit was lifted up. Prayer does change things!

The sign over the church, "Prayer changes things," was just the message I needed. During that summer on Persin, many prisoners were killed. Two were shot for venturing onto forbidden territory. A young boy less than four feet from me was shot in the leg. One day, as we returned from the fields he had stopped to break off an ear of corn. He fell to his knees pleading with the guard to let him live, but the guard walked up to him and shot him through the head before I could intercede for him.

On another occasion a dear friend of mine thought no one was looking. He bent down to pull up a blade of grass and shoved it in his mouth. A shot rang out and he lay at my feet with a huge, gaping hole in

There was no rhyme nor reason for the kill-

the approach of winter, we were transferred to work on the construction of an embankment that was to encircle the island and protect it from flooding. It was to be six yards high and thirty yards thick at the base. The site where we were to work was about four miles from the barracks and we were forced once again to run the four miles with the guards on horseback chasing and whipping us. All of this was to be done on a starvation diet.

The earth for the embankment was carted in crude wheelbarrows from the nearby pastures. The minimum daily work each man was ordered to do was three to six cubic feet. Many collapsed under the strain, and we carried them back to the barracks on our backs or in the wheelbarrows. Sometimes, we were too weak to move those who had fallen and the guards left them there until they died.

One man, a prisoner who had accepted Christ in prison through my ministry, fell and I struggled to carry him to the barracks on my back. But it was just too much. I struggled and managed for a short distance, but could go no further. No one else could help. They, too, were too near death. My friend and brother in Christ died where he lay. If only I could have carried him. I think about him to this day.

Prison brought great friendships between prisoners who shared common depths and sufferings. The best came out in many men, especially Christians. There was great warmth, care and concern for one another. For example, it was common to see a prisoner whose jaw had been smashed by the guards being carefully fed by a fellow-prisoner who broke the bread into unusually tiny bits for him so he could swallow it more easily. Prison brought out the best in most men and there was a strong "brotherhood" together. With Christian prisoners it was even more so.

Mankind's low nature without God hasn't changed.

There were such people when the Egyptian pyramids were built, and when Israel was in captivity in Babylon and during the Enlightenment and in Buchenwald, Siberia and Persin. During this hot, dry summer, anyone who bent down to break off a blade of grass, a leaf of lettuce, anything to eat or chew, was immediately shot without warning. But many of us took the risk in order to live.

The summer was over, and it hadn't rained the whole time. Then it began to rain continuously and the island became a sea of sticky mud. Walking in our home-made rubber shoes, which were open and low, was worse than ever. We patched and mended our ragged clothes to protect ourselves against the coming winter.

The rains continued until the Danube, which had dried up during the summer, again reached its normal level. The lakes and ponds filled again and the road to our work fields became almost impassable.

About this time, the Bulgarian bureaucracy, acting on an idea they picked up from the Russians, decided that snow fences should be built all over the country. We were ordered to weave the snow fences from branches. Their purpose was to prevent snow from spreading out and wetting the fields.

The torrential rains poured as we labored. Our rags were soon soaked through. Almost the whole island was now covered with water. In one month the depth of the river rose from three feet to nine feet.

Our barracks were now sitting in a huge mud puddle thirty inches deep. For weeks we lived in icy river water.

One day, in late November, a light snow mixed with rain began to fall and by evening the ground not covered by water was covered with snow. The following day the blanket of snow became even heavier. Our wet clothes froze. The temperature was down to twenty degrees above zero, but still we had to work on the construction of the snow fences.

The Danube continued to rise and many acres of leeks had yet to be brought in. Wet from living in water, with our clothes frozen hard, we dug the leeks out of the snow with our bare hands, or pulled them out of the icy water, depending on the weather conditions. During the night the water would freeze but the leeks had to be gathered, so we broke the ice with our hands and continued working. Several prisoners died of pneumonia in these months.

"I sink in deep mire, where there is no standing; I am come into deep water, where the floods overflow me" (Psalm 69:2).

The Danube continued to rise throughout December, threatening to flood the entire prison island and several thousand prisoners. The officials were very alarmed about the safety of the farm animals.

Precautions were taken to evacuate the animals if the water continued to rise. But, we the prisoners, weren't to be evacuated under any circumstances. We were less important than the animals! This sounds unbelievable, but we saw preparations made to leave us and evacuate the animals and the guards. After all, it wouldn't have been their "fault" that the flood came, and prisoners were something of which Bulgaria had plenty.

On the smaller island of Sturez, a steel tower was being built as part of an electrification project. The foundation had been dug and the concrete poured. If it filled with water, it could be dangerous, so fifty prisoners including myself were taken to the island to pour concrete into the foundation of the tower. We worked in three shifts while pumps kept the water out of the foundation. Since the work was urgent, the chief guard had two policemen go into the village and obtain bread for us. This was an acknowledgment of the state of semi-starvation in which we were kept. When they had to have emergency work projects done quickly, as in this case, we were given extra rations of bread. That was the one good thing about the rising flood waters. It created so many emergencies they gave us an extra two slices of bread a day! We prayed for more "emergencies."

The Day Before Christmas

On the other side of the island, wooden poles had been washed out by the torrents of flood water, now rising menacingly ever higher, so we were sent to dig new holes and set up the poles again. It was now December 24. We worked in icy, rapidly flowing water up to our waists to retrieve the floating poles and load them onto a raft.

Having loaded one raft I climbed aboard it and began to pole it back to the shore. I was in the middle of the flooded river, when suddenly the raft simply came apart beneath me and I was deposited in the freezing water. I was a half-mile from shore, caught up in the swollen, raging river with a heavy coat and boots on and so frozen, I couldn't move. I was dragged downstream by the current and went under several times, but somehow managed to come back up. I was frozen through by the icy water, the boots dragged me down, the swift current pulled me along.

There was no human way out of this. Death was as certain as it could be. My arms, my legs, my whole body were numb from the icy water. The swift current, the heavy boots and coat were dragging me under again and again. Still I fought my way back to the surface, only to go under again. My strength was completely gone. I gave up struggling. Death had its embrace around me.

With a final breath I cried out, "Lord, help me!" Suddenly a surge of strength shot through my frozen, exhausted body. I began swimming toward the shore with powerful strokes. Incredibly, I was able to pull myself along, heavy, sodden boots and all. It was truly God's strength for I had none left. A strong swimmer

89 •

would have had trouble making it, much less I in my condition. Yet, I could see I was making progress. I said over and over "Thank You, Lord." Later, I remembered that beautiful hymn:

Though sometimes He leads through waters deep.
Trials fall across the way.
Though sometimes the path seems rough and steep.
See His footsteps all the way.

Those watching from the shore had already written me off as dead and had turned away and gone about their work. After all, life was so cheap, one prisoner more or less meant nothing. We had seen so many die, death was commonplace.

I struggled closer and closer to the shore. Finally, I could see the shore and saw two figures in black. They were nuns. At that time a trial against Catholic priests and nuns had just concluded, and they, too, had been convicted of espionage. More than fifty priests and nuns were condemned to prison and two Bishops and two priests were executed. The two nuns before me were floundering in the mud at the river bank while a woman guard commanded them to keep going. The guard brutally kicked one of the nuns, causing her to fall flat where she sank into the soft, oozing mud. She pulled herself up with great effort.

The village of Belene was about a mile and a half from us. It was Christmas. The bells of the church began to ring out with the glad tidings of the Christian faith. At the moment the bells began pealing, the two nuns down at the river bank were floundering and sinking in the mud without anyone to help them and I, an evangelical pastor, had just used my last ounce of strength to swim ashore and lay exhausted. The bells seemed to be saying, "God is born in the form of a man. God is revealing Himself through His Child."

I'll never forget that Christmas. I was laying exhausted and the two nuns were sinking deeper into the mud. We stopped our struggling and listened. It was dark and freezing cold. I was almost a solid block of ice. The bells could be heard faintly far off in the distance ringing out the message of the Saviour's birth.

Tears rolled down my cheeks as I lay there. They were tears of joy because I had not drowned and tears of sorrow because neither the nuns nor I were here for any crimes we had committed. We were here for His sake — He who was born in a stable on that night so long ago.

I thought of the martyrs of the past: of the mothers whose children Herod had killed; the saints who were stoned to death; the thousands burned to death, bound to stakes; the thousands thrown to the lions. Church history is stained with the blood of thousands of Christian martyrs because they had received God's Son for whom those bells now tolled. These martyrs were not blind fanatics, but men and women with a faith that lasted unto death. The faith which overcomes death has no fear. Instead there is joy and a song! Martyrs! I relived the past as the bells rang. I looked at the nuns. Tears were coursing down their cheeks as well. We wept. We said not a word, but we understood each other.

When the bells stopped, the present reality came rushing back, but the Voice of God spoke to my heart, "This they have done to My children through the ages and this they do to you for My sake."

CHRISTMASES IN PRISON

That Christmas and twelve others came and passed in cold, frozen cells. When I was in solitary confinement on Christmas day, I spent the day thinking of Ruth, Paul and Rhoda, wondering what they were doing that day, if they were well. I never permitted myself the luxury of thinking I would ever see them again. I had long ago abandoned all hope of ever being with them again. So on those thirteen Christmases, whether in a cell with others or in solitary confinement, I never thought of seeing them again. It was enough to make a man go mad and many had.

One Christmas in solitary confinement, I devoted to making myself "Christmas cards" out of pieces of paper. I knew very well I would never receive a Christmas card from the prison commandant!

I made one which I labelled "from Ruth," one "from Rhoda" and one "from Paul." I lay in the cell that Christmas looking at the lovely cards from "home." I told myself, "MERRY CHRISTMAS, HARALAN." The Judas-hole slid open and the guard looked in. He must have thought I had gone mad and was now talking to myself.

When the Judas-hole had been closed, tears flooded down my cheeks as the total despair caused by missing my loved ones struck me anew. I quickly took hold of myself. "Haralan, you've got to stop this," I lectured myself.

Other Christmases I spent trying to lift the spirits of fellow prisoners. This was the worst day of the year for everyone. Men who were buoyant and strong all year, often lapsed into deep despair on Christmas Day.

After three or four Christmases came and passed, I began to spend entire Christmas days as days devoted to being a prison pastor to the men and trying to help them meet the spiritual crises in their lives which were especially acute on that day.

The main barracks at Persin were built directly on the ground, but the waters of the river had not yet reached them as they were protected by the retaining wall we had built at such cost in human lives during the summer. We had also built an embankment thirty yards long, twelve yards wide and two yards high, and on this we had built two barracks. One night, we were awakened in the barracks by the noise of shouts. Someone yelled, "The river has broken through the retaining wall! Run for your lives!"

As we ran out of the barracks and into the yard the water was already waist deep and rising fast. Three or four thousand men struggled through the icy, brackish water to the two barracks built higher up on the embankment, which had been built for only a hundred and twenty men! We were so jammed that we could hardly move, but we just huddled together. There we stood without guards, for they had abandoned us and were on higher ground on the other side. The water rose steadily higher.

There was no attempt to rescue us. If the water continued to rise at least several hundred men would die, for many were simply too weak to swim. I prayed, asking the other Christians among the prisoners to pray with me. At last the rising waters stopped and we knew we were saved. I thanked God for this.

Since there were no guards present, the informers and members of the "Cultural Society" were left without protection. The non-Christian prisoners who had suffered so much from the informers found a chance to take their revenge on them. What followed was brutal. Throughout the night, safe from guards, the beating of the informers continued and when daylight came, many were bloody and injured. I tried to stop the angry prisoners, but their fury at those who betrayed them was beyond control. I was roughly pushed aside and told, "Pastor, stay out of this!"

Finally, when the water receded and it was safe the guards and the prison director returned. When the director learned what had happened, he cursed and raged and swore to take revenge. Since no one would confess to taking a part in the beating of the informers, the prison director selected fourteen men at random to be the victims of his revenge.

These unfortunate men were placed on a pontoon, rowed to the middle of the river and anchored there, stranded in the middle of the river. It was bitterly cold. They had only very light prison clothes, no food and only river water to drink. A guard was posted on the shore to watch them. They remained there two whole weeks in terrible cold and suffering. On the second day there came a strong, icy wind and the temperature sank to below zero. The fourteen men stamped their feet and hopped and jumped about as much as they could to maintain the circulation of their blood. On the fifth day, the prison director took a motor boat into the river and cruised around the pontoon with the fourteen freezing, dying men, mocking them in the vilest language imaginable.

The rest of us also had to pay a price for the men who beat the informers. We were all ordered out to the river bank and forced at bayonet point to stand for ten days, exposed to the now sub-zero cold and fierce winds sweeping down the river, with nothing to eat or drink and no possibility of lying down. It was so cold that even the swollen, raging Danube now began to freeze over. It was a horrible, nightmarish scene.

All around me men pathetically tried to get warm. One shouted, "Jump around! It will keep you warm." Many started jumping in a desperate struggle against the deadly cold. Next to me, an older man began jumping. I cautioned him not to use up his energy this way. He continued and the next day fell at my feet. I tried to help him, but he died in my arms. His body lay frozen at my feet for several days before the guards came to take it away.

During the confusion of the flood, one young prisoner managed to get away in a boat and rowed to the mainland without being seen. He walked about 22 miles to the city of Levski before he was caught and brought back to Persin. As punishment for escaping, the young prisoner was locked in the small kitchen of one of the huts which was so cold that it had ice covering half the walls. When he was let out several days later, he was so frozen he could hardly walk. He had almost frozen to death and had to have both frost-bitten feet amputated.

Finally, after two weeks, the fourteen men on the pontoon were brought back to the barracks. Their feet had frozen and they had black spots visible on their skin. One man had to have his frozen toes amputated. We were allowed to go back to our barracks after ten days at the frozen river banks.

SLAVE LABOR AT PERSIN

The flood took a heavy toll of livestock on the island. That's what really distressed the prison director. It showed that the only way to avoid endangering the prisoners and animals was to raise the level of the island, so we were ordered to carry sand and stone by barrow to the area which was to be raised. Freezing and half-starved, we were ordered to dig up thirteen cubic feet of frozen earth every day and carry it a hundred yards to the new location.

After we had finished with the raising of the land, we were put on a wood-sawing detail on the island of Barzina, just north of Persin. Barzina is a little over four miles long and two or three hundred yards wide. The trees there are unbelievably thick and tall. Every morning we carried our pontoon to the water's edge, and every night we carried it and the tree trunks we had cut back up the hill! After we got the tree trunks on land we had to carry them on our backs and shoulders a mile or more to the building site. It took about 20 hunger-weakened men to carry the tree trunks which were 45 to 60 feet long and up to two feet in diameter. Many times, I fell under the terrible weight of the trees. Dying men cursed — and others prayed. I thought, *How foolish! If the communists want labor they should feed the prisoners. Then they would get much more work per man.* But they never seemed to think of that.

Heavy snows came and Persin settled into the great, white freezing silence of winter. Only bent, broken dark figures could be seen moving with great pain, under the heavy load of felled trees. Those who collapsed lay where they fell, their bodies turning black and frozen hard as stone. When their bodies were finally removed, their arms and legs remained frozen in the grotesque form in which they had fallen. We who lived envied them their escape.

At last, spring came, reviving our spirits. Nettles and other edible greens began to appear through the snow in the forests. We also ate frogs, snakes, turtles and field rats. I will never forget the taste of field rats. Rat meat is strange, sweet-sour and very stringy with tendons. But we were so starved, the rats were a feast.

* * *

"The sorrows of death compassed me, and the pains of hell gat hold upon me: I found trouble and sorrow. Then called I upon the name of the Lord; O Lord, I beseech thee, deliver my soul" (Psalm 116:3, 4).

On March 5, 1953, we noticed during inspection that the guards wore black bands on their coat lapels. The chief of the barracks announced with a quivering voice that Comrade Stalin had died. All guards and Cultural Society members went around with mournful expressions. For most prisoners, however, Stalin's death was cause for jubilation. We tried to hide our feelings, but the informers knew who stood where, and the guards went to work on those who had shook hands or not looked sufficiently sad during the announcement. Many men were badly beaten that night because they didn't look mournful enough.

One old man who faced life imprisonment laughed when he heard the news, and laughed madly throughout the vicious beating he received.

After Stalin's death, the guards became worse. The reason was their own insecurity. Stalin had been more than a leader to them; he was a higher being whom they worshiped. Now that their god had died, their emotions of anger and fear had to be expressed somehow. We were conveniently at hand, so we were the victims. We prisoners were blamed for all wrong as though we had caused Stalin's death.

Here I must say that I have found in the free world the feeling that, certainly things were bad under Stalin, as even Khrushchev confessed, but things since Stalin have improved. This is totally untrue. The punishment and suffering became less extensive for a while, then more clever and subtle and dangerous. We experienced it immediately. Today, millions in communist lands are suffering as badly as we did, only it is more subtle torture. Children are taken from Christian parents for life. Is this not torture? In the communist world today, Christians are tortured and imprisoned. True Christian leaders die in prison of "natural causes." The overall suffering is worse today in many communist lands than it was under Stalin.

INTO THE DEATH CHAMBER

Our torture became like a pendulum. It swung to less persecution for a while, then back again.

One hundred prisoners were selected, including myself, to form a "punishment brigade" and we were put in special barracks. Every day the punishment became more severe. One day we were ordered to bring out all our belongings. These were searched and all food given to the gypsies in another barracks. Even our daily bread ration was denied us. Then we were marched to a warehouse, ordered to take off our pants and overcoats, and given ragged and threadbare clothes in exchange. The pants were so tight we were not able to button them, and we had to hold them up with one hand. The purpose of all this was to destroy the last bit of our self-respect, but we marched proudly through the yard with our heads held high — and our pants held up.

On April 20 we were shut up in a room and put on a starvation diet of ten ounces of bread and a few spoonsful of bean soup from which the beans had been strained. Here we sat day and night with nothing to do and barely enough food to keep us alive. It soon became clear that we were to starve to death. Time was our fearful enemy.

The clock stopped.

We sat completely still, the utter silence being broken only by the labored breathing of doomed men. We were left totally alone, no food, little water. One week passed, then two. Suddenly, we would hear a noise and every weakened head turned. I realize my frequent use of the word "suddenly" may sound monotonous, but it can't be helped. Clumsy as it is, it describes the situation. In the damp world and stagnation of our sepulchre, the guards would from time to time *suddenly* invade the cell to remind us that, unlike the normal dead, we could be tormented again and again, physically and mentally, subtly and brutally, alone or together, day and night.

Perhaps our physical suffering, the lack of food, water and air clouded our consciousness through those long weeks, but it seemed the world stopped as we sat literally waiting for death.

Finally, on May 8, we in the "punishment brigade" were to be transferred to Barracks Number Two, while the concentration camp prisoners took our place in Number One. Separated from the main body of prisoners, we marched the four and one-half miles to Barracks Number Two, with an escort of guards on horseback who chased us as usual with long leather whips.

I sensed a dark object racing toward my face from the side as the jagged end of a long whip tore across my face leaving a stream of blood. "Faster! Faster!" shouted the guards on their horses. I remembered in a flash Jesus being beaten with the whip and in a moment of lucid thought, between gasps of breath, prayed, "Lord, help me to bear it for Your name's sake!" For two hours I ran, staggered and fell along with the biting lash of the great black whips cutting through prison clothing and flesh like a knife through butter. After two hours, the haggard, beaten "punishment brigade," with me in the rear, reached our barracks and fell exhausted and bleeding to the floor.

Barracks Number Two lay well above the floodwaters of the Danube and was surrounded by barbed wire. On the east and west sides were high towers manned day and night. Near the entrance gate we saw a sign, loosely translated: "Man is something to be proud of" — a quotation from Maxim Gorki. I was struck by the irony of this quotation here in a communist prison, where thousands of men were treated like animals. But the words themselves contain a real truth. God's Word teaches that man is the crown of creation. There is nothing on the face of the earth greater than man. It is strange that men who refuse to receive the Creator and who don't consider a human being to be of any value had written those words on the wall.

The gate opened and we were let in. When we looked behind us we saw another quotation by Maxim Gorki: "If the enemy doesn't surrender, he must be annihilated."

I thought about the contradiction in the two phrases, reflecting the division in the mind of the writer. By this, one can understand the chasm between communism in theory and communism in practice. The first quotation showed communist theory in its effort to create an earthly paradise. The second phrase showed the harsh reality. On the one hand, man is something to be proud of; on the other, he is an enemy who must be annihilated!

This is the difference between communism in theory and communism in reality. Within several minutes, four or five thousand men had been gathered inside the barbed wire enclosure. We were called enemies, because we hadn't surrendered and hadn't permitted the communist ideals to triumph over our minds and hearts. Communism demands complete conformity and subservience. We had refused to conform and were the vilest enemy. According to the words on the guardhouse, these men, at one time, had been something to be proud of. In reality the quotation is a good argument against communism. It hurt us that only we, the enemies of communism, could read them.

After several days, we discovered that prisoners from other brigades were digging a deep hole near our barracks. We watched the progress of the deepening, widening hole with curiosity. We had no idea what its purpose was. When it was completed, a group of workmen began building in the deep cavity under the direction of a former building contractor. Then the word came by prison grapevine that this was a special punishment pit being prepared to accommodate the penal brigade — us! Looking at the forbidding pit, I asked God for special strength. Little did I know I was to spend the next 9 months in the almost airless pit jammed with starving men fighting for every breath. With all I had seen and experienced of man's inhumanity to man I was still surprised at man's creative and satanic genius at finding new ways to torture his fellow-man.

When I preach salvation today I do it with a new fervor. For 13 years I lived with everyday experience of how low men can sink without God. Man has the capacity to rise to the greatest spiritual heights but he also has the capacity to sink to the lowest, most vile levels. No animal has this "range." Only man.

NINE MONTHS IN THE PIT

"And they took him, and cast him into the pit: and the pit was empty, there was no water in it" (Genesis 37:24).

The pit was a huge hole in the ground about 10 feet deep. The sides of the pit were lined with heavy timbers to prevent caving in and the ceiling was made of thick wooden beams stretching from one side of the hole to the other. In between the beams were planks of wood with the small cracks daubed with clay. It was air tight. There were no windows, of course, and no air vents. The "door" was a "trap door" in the ceiling, 20 inches wide. It was the only air inlet. The pit was divided by upright beams and iron bars into two parts, with a passageway between. On one side were one-man cells, measuring 9 by 6 feet. On the other was one big room, 60 by 12 feet.

After it was completed we were told that we were to be punished in a new way. (The prison grapevine had told us in advance.) All 100 of us were led out single file and "dropped" through the trap door onto the damp, sandy floor of the pit. On one side of the passageway stood a barrel of drinking water, on the other side was the barrel which served as the toilet for 100 men. The floor was a layer of cold, damp sand. In the totally dark, hot, airless hole, we soon removed all our clothes except our undershorts, and lay on the cool sand gasping for air.

There we awaited death. The only indication of time was the morning and evening meal consisting of our bread ration and "soup" water with not even a bean in it, and a smaller amount than before.

The Incident of the Bean

Once, by accident or oversight, a single bean was left floating in the "soup" of one man. What rejoicing by the man in whose bowl it was found! You would have thought it was a huge roast of beef. But only someone who has been in such a prison can know the significance and meaning of discovering one bean floating in watery "soup." We all rejoiced with him over the bean. Men who have nothing will grasp at any straw.

It was now Spring, and the accumulated heat of the airless pit became a stifling oven, fed by the still, decayed air, heavy with the heat, perspiration and odor of 100 bodies gasping for air in a deadly struggle for the next breath.

After several days, some of the older prisoners became unconscious. We beat on the trap door to attract attention, and when the guards opened the door and lowered themselves into the mass of wriggling bodies they found 10 prisoners unconscious. These men were taken outside to be revived. As soon as they came to they were thrown back in again. I lay on the floor of the pit, burying my face deeply in the sand, trying to breath the air trapped in the loose sand.

The next day we had to beat on the door three times as our friends fainted in the heat or through lack of oxygen. It was clear all would soon die under present conditions. But they didn't want us to "escape" them that easily through death. They always wanted us to die their way, not ours. So the following day we were removed from the pit and returned to the punishment barracks for several days while workmen made ventilation holes in the roof of the dungeon. We looked like the "Legion of the Dead." Our brief respite was soon over and again we were lowered into the pit, one by one. While there was a little more air, we still fought for every breath and the pit was again full of the sounds of 100 men gasping for breath.

We remained there day and night through May and June in total blackness. We had all lost weight and looked like pallid skeletons by then.

But our labor was needed. In early July we were taken from the dungeon each morning and put to work filling a small lake with dirt. When the other prisoners saw us emerging from the pit like sick moles from the earth, they were horrified by our appearance. They were in such bad shape themselves, we must have looked horrible. We were so weak that we could move only a few shovelsful of dirt at a time in the wheel barrows, but the fresh air and sunshine were a blessing.

During July the authorities began building an embankment around the island at great speed. The prisoners who could not do two days work in one day were thrown into the pit with us, though we were already crowded with wasted bodies. The new arrivals were put in the big room, while we "old-timers," all 100 of us, were placed in the one-man cells. In the mornings the new prisoners were taken out to work, and in the evenings brought back to the dungeon, but we were kept behind, spending every day and night in total darkness, except for occasional shafts of light when the trap-door was opened and closed.

There were 17 of us in each stifling hot "one-man" cell! We were literally piled on top of one another. Yet, living as starved moles deep in the earth, there was an amazing spirit of brotherly love among us.

With 17 men in a one-man cell, it was impossible to lie down. Sleep became impossible, so I said to the men, "We can't all sleep at once. We must sleep in shifts. Half should sleep on the floor while the other half crowd against the walls in the smallest space possible. When those sleeping finish, they can crowd together and those standing can sleep."

They accepted my suggestion and half stretched out and slept and half stood packed tightly against the bars as they slept. In this way, we all managed to get some sleep, fitful though it was.

As the weeks passed, we began to be summoned, one by one, before the DS and asked to become informers. My turn came and I entered the office of our former barracks chief, Boris Miteff. There was another young man present. Miteff said "Comrade Popov, I would like you to meet Comrade Tritchkov." The alarm bells rang in my head. They had addressed me as "Comrade." I knew I had to be very careful.

Tritchkov asked me how my family was, then said, "Comrade Popov, we have decided to free you from the pit, since we feel you will be more sensible and obliging in the future."

I couldn't believe my ears! Hope welled up within me, even though I fought it, knowing there was a condition.

No more torture . . . no more stifling hot pit. I thought. Then Tritchkov continued, "We only want you to do us a little favor. When we let you go, we want you to go to the barracks and give us a written report on the condition of the prisoners there and what they talk about."

So that's it, I thought.

This amounted to becoming an informer and collaborator. The seemingly innocent favor was to cover what would have been my spiritual surrender. They had temporarily broken my will physically at the trial, but they had never brainwashed or "reformed" me. I had held out this long and I was determined not to give in now. Yet I knew this was the most decisive choice in my life; either to accept the invitation and be freed from the pit so that I could come out in the fresh air and the sun, or to decline to do the little "favor," and remain faithful to my God and retain the confidence of my fellow prisoners and probably die in the pit. There was no other option, and under the present condition, death was only a matter of time. I had begun to black out from time to time in the pit, clear signs of lack of air and a collapsing respiratory system.

For a moment, I closed my eyes in silent prayer. The two men awaited my answer. Suddenly God's Word came to me: ". . . that the trial of your faith, being much more precious than of gold that perisheth, though it be tried with fire, might be found unto praise and honor and glory at the appearing of Jesus Christ" (I Peter 1:7).

It was completely clear to me then that if I said

"yes" I would become an apostate and lose my faith and my hope in God.

I gave a concise answer: "No." That was all I said.

Tritchkov's cordial expression immediately disappeared. He said, "Popov." (The title "Comrade" was now suddenly dropped.) "Don't answer too quickly. This is a serious matter. I warn you, think a little more about it. You do want to see your family again, don't you?"

I answered, "You know that I am a pastor. I believe in God and serve Him. I am a pastor to these men. And now you want me to report to you all they tell me. Never could I do that." I went on, "Do what you want to me and this body. It is but clay. But I will never deny my faith."

Tritchkov clenched his fists and roared, "Then you will rot in that pit! You will never get out!" I had heard those words before and God had overridden them once and could do so again.

So it was back to the pit. In August, dysentery struck us. It lasted for a month and left us like skeletons covered with skin. Never could I describe the inferno that was the pit. Men lay like the dead, not moving and gasping for air. The horrible smell from the overflowing cans was overpowering. Almost total darkness 24 hours a day. Seventeen men in one-man cells. Fed only "soup" which was flavored water. It was like a scene out of Dante's "Inferno." The sounds of men gasping for one more breath filled the pit. How long could this go on? We had already been down here for six months! Some, who lapsed into unconsciousness and then slipped into death, were the fortunate ones.

At the end of August, a new prison director took charge and one day as the soup was poured into our cups, one of the men shouted, "There's a bean here!" You can't imagine what that one bean meant. At last we had a bean or two in the "soup."

Apparently, we were more valuable alive than dead. They needed our labor and began releasing us, early in September, for hard labor, a few at a time. On November 30, I was released. I had been in the darkened, steaming pit for nine months! Only God kept me alive.

Tritchkov's prediction — like the earlier ones — that I would rot there was not fulfilled. Our lives and destinies do not depend on human ambitions and predictions, but on a higher will and power. God opened the door of the pits. Now it was back to the regular routine in prison.

My Work As a Prison Pastor

Conditions in prison changed little by little for the better. We had a little more food, but still not enough for a grown man. The physical beatings and torture became less frequent, but the "brainwashing" efforts increased. The emphasis changed to more subtle psychological torture. During all my years of imprisonment, I had used every occasion possible to serve as a "Prison Pastor" to the prisoners.

Since I had been removed from my pulpit, I was determined my pulpit would be wherever I was.

With the improvement in food and the new strength it gave me, I found I could increase my ministry in prison; and I had more energy to witness and minister to the men. Up until this time, I was too weak from fighting for life. With the easing of conditions somewhat, my ministry started in a much increased scale. I am sure the communists didn't intend this, but it was the result of new-found energy. Soon, I was running a regular "church" in prison. My "congregation" were men who were in dire need, spiritual and physical. My "church" was a cell, the prison exercise yard, or anywhere we could meet. We always had to camouflage the purpose of our gathering. God abundantly blessed this ministry and time and time again, a prisoner would say to me, "Pastor, I've been listening and thinking about what you've been telling us and I want to serve Christ, too." These were the moments that I lived for and I had the joy of bringing many to Christ in the various prisons but especially there at Persin.

Where a man expressed his interest in Christ, we would pray together wherever we were. If it were in the fields where we were working, we would go down on our knees, pretend we were looking closely at something on the ground, but actually we were praying.

One day, while I was praying with a prisoner in the field, a guard rode up on his horse and shouted, "What are you men doing there?"

I replied, "Looking at the harvest."

He didn't know I meant a *spiritual* harvest!

Men in prison are at the end of themselves. In normal life men have wives and children and jobs. This, plus material things, can dull a man's sense of his need for God. But in prison all this was taken away. Men had time to think. Their values became clear in prison and many genuinely realized their need of God. It was a very fruitful field for a Prison Pastor.

But more than anything else, I needed a Bible or Testament or gospel for my ministry with the men. The Word of God held the answer to their needs, but I didn't have a Bible and it was impossible even to hope to get one. I prayed, "Lord, these men need Your Word. These are eternal souls. God, I'm doing my very best but they need Your Word." I left it in God's hands. No prison bars can stop Him. The impossible is the possible with God! So I left it with God.

"Thy words were found, and I did eat them: and thy word was unto me the joy and rejoicing of mine heart" (Jeremiah 15:16).

One day I noticed that Stoil, the man whose bed was next to mine, had something in his hands. I couldn't tell what it was, but it looked like a little book. Then I saw what he was doing. Stoil was tearing a page out of the book in which to roll a cigarette. To my astonishment I saw that it was a New Testament!

I had not seen a Scripture portion for five years! Instinctively I grabbed it from Stoil and looked at it. Stoil started to grab it back as tears flowed down my cheeks. He stopped, caught with surprise at what it obviously meant to me.

"Stoil," I asked, "Where did you get this book?"

"When we were transferred here from the first barracks area, I found it in a trash can."

I said, "Stoil, please give me the Book."

"No," he answered firmly, "I'm reading it." He grabbed it from my hands.

But I knew he wanted the thin paper only for use as cigarette paper! I couldn't bear the thought of God's Word which I had not seen for five years being used as cigarette paper.

"Stoil, I will give you all the money I have for the book." At this particular time we were able to keep a little money on hand at times to buy from the prison canteen.

When I offered Stoil all the money I had his eyes widened. Then he brightened and answered: "Pastor, since you want it so much you may have it. Here, take it!" Then I held it! God's Word! I wept before the men and they turned their heads so as not to embarrass me.

For five years I had starved physically, but I had starved even more spiritually, and I can tell you the spiritual hunger is more painful than the physical. Now I began to take the advice of Ezekiel 3:3 ". . . cause thy belly to eat, and fill thy bowels with this roll that I give thee. . . . Then did I eat."

I had given my life to God in 1926. From that day until the day I was arrested, God's Word had been my inseparable daily companion. Then, abruptly, I had been cut off from it for five years. I offered Stoil all my money for the New Testament, but I would have given him my arm or leg if he had asked for it! That's what God's Word meant to me then — and now.

What an indescribable loss it is to be without a Bible or Testament! During my whole time in prison I felt an emptiness and sharp, almost physical pain at being denied the Word of God. I had, of course, read God's Word my whole Christian life, and knew verses and longer portions, but because of the torture and beatings I had been through and the long time I had been separated from God's Word, I had forgotten certain parts. Strangely, torture often has the effect of clouding the memory. I noticed this effect very often.

I knew I wouldn't be able to keep the New Testament for long. Eventually the prison guards would find and destroy it. But as long as I remained here on the island I could hide it out in the fields, in the straw and hay. Each day I hid it in a different place so they wouldn't notice a pattern. After hiding it in straw and hay I began to dig holes, put up a marker of some kind and dig it up to read. By all means, I knew I had to keep it in the fields because our cells were often searched. But since my best chance to read it was late at night in my cell, I took the risk of taking it back to the cell with me, praying all the while there would be no surprise inspection that night. This also gave me more opportunities to read to the prisoners.

MEMORIZING 47 CHAPTERS

Realizing I wouldn't have the Testament for long, I decided to memorize as much of it as possible. I began to "eat" God's Word, memorizing many verses every day. Everywhere I went I had the Testament with me. I always found occasion to study it. First, I memorized 1 Peter, then Ephesians, 1 John, the gospel of John, Romans 1, 5 and 8, 1 Corinthians 13 and 14, and 2 Corinthians 5. Forty-seven chapters in all.

When I was later moved to a regular prison, it was impossible to hide the Testament any longer. But by then I was almost a "walking New Testament." Now with God's Word I began greatly to enlarge my ministry to my fellow prisoners. During the years ahead, God prospered my ministry in prison as I used every possible opportunity to minister to the men about me. Of course, it had to be "underground" ministry, for it was punishable by beatings or starvation.

It was particularly dangerous work, as I never knew who the informers in our midst were. I wondered what to do about the problem of informers. If I were cautious, the men would sense I was fearful and my Christian influence would be harmed. Then I decided, "Well, the informers need the Word of God, too!" Let them hear it also. If they talk, they talk.

From that day on I never permitted myself to think of the dangers of informers. Of course, many times I would be called to the prison director's office and told, "Popov, we know you held a secret religious meeting in your cell! We know that. When will you ever learn?"

Then I would be taken to a special punishment cell for a week of water only. On one occasion, on my release from the punishment cell, the prison director ordered me back to his office and said, "What is it with you, Popov? Do you enjoy the punishment cell? This is the sixteenth time you've been in it." I replied, "You can never deny a bird to sing or a fish to swim. It is natural. I am a pastor. My entire life is given to bringing men to God. And, whatever you do with me, I cannot stop doing what my God has given me to do. You have taken me from my pulpit and put me here, and here I shall do my work."

As soon as I had finished saying that, he roared, "Take this prisoner back to the punishment cell!"

I continued using every occasion to teach about Jesus

Christ to my fellow prisoners. Birthdays were wonderful opportunities because we could sing together and in the guise of offering best wishes, I could preach the men God's Word. Birthdays were such wonderful opportunities to worship God together, that often each prisoner had 4 or 5 "birthdays" a year! Many were deeply interested and gave their lives to Christ. Others were embittered against God for their imprisonment. I could only give them God's Word and depend upon the Holy Spirit to complete the work.

PREACHING BY PRISON TELEGRAPH

In prison we had developed a "Prison Telegraph." One existed in most prisons because in prisons, communication with one another is very important. This was the way prisoners passed news along the "prison grapevine." The prison telegraph consisted of a crude "Morse code." One tap on the wall stood for the letter "A." Two taps were "B." Three taps were "C" and so on, all the way through the alphabet. To say something with the letter "V" in it took ages! Yet, it worked.

One day I heard the familiar cry, "Prisoner Popov, step out." An informer had reported on my underground prayer meetings or Bible teaching classes again. By now, it was an old routine. Off to the prison director's office and from there to the punishment cell for a week or two.

The punishment cells were a row of small isolation or solitary confinement cells. They took me this time to Cell 27 in the middle of the cell block.

Left alone, I had an idea. If the Prison Telegraph could be used to spread rumors and news, why couldn't it be used to spread the Gospel? I took my tin drinking cup and began tapping on the wall and waited. Sure enough, in just a few moments, there came a tapping sound from the other side.

"What is your name?" I tapped.

"M-I-T-S-H-E-V" he replied.

"How long have you been there?" I tapped.

"Three weeks," he tapped back.

I soon developed a special "technique" for tapping. If it were discovered by the guards, I would be stopped. So, I stood up in the cell with my back leaning on the cell wall, as if I were resting and tapped with the cup in my hand behind me. This way I could keep my eye on the Judas-hole and immediately stop if I heard or saw the little door over the Judas-hole open. I told Mitschev to listen because I had something very important to tell him.

He tapped back that he was ready.

I asked him if he were a born-again believer in Christ. "No," he replied.

"Have you heard that Christ died for our sins?"

"Only in the Orthodox Church when I was a boy," Mitshev replied.

"Listen," I tapped, "because I want to tell you what Christ can do for you."

Then, for the next three days, interrupted only by sleep, I "preached" a message of God's love and Christ's salvation to Mitshev. After we stopped for a night, Mitshev would start by tapping, a question such as, "But, Pastor, how can my sins be gone? I don't understand." This was good! Mitshev was thinking.

On the fourth day, Mitshev tapped back, "I am ready now to believe on Jesus, pray for me. I am ready to accept Christ." I told him to get on his knees in his cell and I would get on mine in my cell and we would pray together. A few minutes later, Mitshev tapped back. "I do thank God. I have given my life to Him." After his conversion, I built his faith for 3 more days until I was taken back to my regular cell. All of this was by tapping with a tin cup. Not one audible word was ever said.

I never saw Mitshev, but I knew he had found Christ.

After this, I tapped the Gospel almost up to the day

of my release and came to welcome visits to this punishment cell because of the opportunity it gave me to witness to those in the next cells by tapping the Gospel. In the many years to come I witnessed and preached the Gospel very often by Prison Telegraph tapping with a tin cup on the cell walls. Using my "back against the wall, eyes on the Judas-hole" technique, I never once was caught.

Many men whom I never saw told me on the Prison Telegraph they had gained new strength and faith in God. For this I praise God.

After the New Year of 1954 came the most cold winter months. The temperature dropped to twenty degrees below freezing and the snow piled up to a depth of three feet. We had to work as usual. We shoveled snow all day, then watched the blizzard cover the roads again. One night was so cold that even though we wrapped ourselves up in blankets and pelts, many of us had frostbitten hands, feet and noses and ears.

In spite of the swift current, the Danube froze. Two young boys tried to escape even though all tracks were visible in the snow. They were caught, handcuffed and put into the punishment cell. The handcuffs had spiked teeth on the insides which cut into the flesh at the slightest movement.

It was still bitter cold, and after ten days, the hands and feet of the two boys were blue and in danger of freezing. The boys screamed for help and a doctor was called, but all help was useless. They were taken to the hospital where the doctor amputated every one of their fingers. Unable to work any more, they were transferred to a prison on the mainland.

A veterinarian was punished along with the boys. He did not have handcuffs on so only his feet were frozen. The doctor had to amputate everything but his heels. He was released after a couple of months and was able to walk again with the help of crutches.

At the end of March, the snow melted and the ice on the Danube began to break up. The lower part of Persin became flooded and Barracks Number two was affected. The water remained on the island a long time and all work had to be stopped. It was a wonderful opportunity for the prisoners to rest, and a wonderful opportunity to witness for Christ without the interruption of hard labor.

One day I felt a sudden pain in my right hip which the doctor diagnosed as a severe attack of sciatica. He said that the joints themselves were infected. The pains grew more unbearable each day. I was given Novocain and aspirin, but nothing seemed to help. It felt as if a knife had cut through flesh and bone. During July the summer heat began and the pain in my leg was reduced by sunbathing. I managed to get around on crutches.

Until the end of August, I rested. Then I was taken to a hospital and given special medicine sent to me from Sweden by way of my brother. Gradually the pain subsided. I was able to walk with a cane, and felt pain only when I stood on my bad leg.

On October 17, the sciatica pain suddenly left me. Ruth later wrote to me that on just this day, she had awakened early. It was the day of our wedding anniversary, and as she prayed, her thoughts were naturally on me and my illness. Ruth doesn't find it easy to cry but she cried then, and her fervent prayer was heard, for I was healed the same day. Answers to prayers sometimes come faster than we dare to believe.

At the end of November, I was released from the hospital, but I still couldn't work. On February 26, 1955, together with 50 others who were also unable to work, I was put aboard a box car on a train which would take us to different prisons in Bulgaria.

The joy of leaving Persin was almost as overwhelming as when I was later freed. What memories I had left back on that island — the bad times and the good times. Especially was I thrilled to know I was leaving behind many prisoners who had found Christ through my ministry.

Together with the 50 other disabled veterans of Persin I strode down the side streets of Belene to the station, some three miles away. Though we were ill, our spirits were high. Anything was better than Persin, we thought.

The prison at Varna where I was taken was several miles outside the city and surrounded by vineyards. It was often called "the monastery" because of its distinctive red brick exterior.

At Varna there was a large sign which read, "Today's prisons in the People's Republic of Bulgaria do not serve for punishment but for retraining." I had already proved I was not a good subject for retraining.

The superintendent of the prison was called Tchipaiev, after the hero of a Russian film. To this day I don't know his real name. Tall and thin, with a swollen face, he was known and feared as one for torturing prisoners rather than "retraining" them. Seldom did we see him sober. Later, I heard he died from alcoholism.

There were no cells in this prison and we were taken to a big dormitory which had previously been furnished with 10 beds on each side with a wooden table in the middle. The beds had been replaced with wooden bunks and now offered accommodation for 25 prisoners, but we numbered between 40 and 50. The table was taken out and some had to make their beds on the floor.

I shall never forget how it felt to wash off the dirt from Persin! It was like a snake changing its skin. To take a shower, to wash my hands before I ate, to sleep in a bunk rather than on a cement floor — this was so wonderful! And so *temporary,* as I was to learn later.

We were given no work, so I had time to read my New Testament more than usual and memorized large portions, aware I couldn't hide it forever. I was in a desperate "race" to memorize as many chapters as possible before the inevitable discovery and confiscation. One unpleasant innovation at Varna was the frequent propaganda lectures. Almost every day, a number of the "Cultural Society" lectured us for a couple of hours on rehabilitation. The prisoners hated it. There were such "exciting" topics as "The History of the Soviet Union Communist Party" and "The History of the Bulgarian Communist Party."

We were given communist newspapers, parts of which were marked to be read. I read everything but those parts. We were forced to read editorials, articles on agriculture and on the construction of factories — on everything which promoted communism and its goals.

Once we read that a delegation of Bulgarian communists had visited China. It was reported that they greatly praised the communists' victorious crusade in China. Among other things, the article reported about rice cultivation there. It seems the communists there had such extraordinary grains of rice that one could reap 100 pounds of rice from every three square feet. A friend and I calculated that if we poured a hundred pounds of rice on an area of three square feet, there would be a layer six inches thick! I read this discovery to the barracks full of men and all roared with laughter except one. We then knew who the "resident informer" was.

The food got better, and we could buy certain things we wanted in the canteen. My brother, Ladin, who had finished five years of imprisonment, and was now serving as an underground pastor, often brought food parcels.

I didn't care about the communist's motives for giving us more food. I was only grateful for the added strength to carry out my work for God in the prison.

Another significant development was a week of meetings between the Secret Service and the Prison Welfare Department. Prisoners were called in for new hearings, usually a sign that release was imminent. A first group — those arrested in connection with Tito's break with Russia — had been released in 1955. In May, 1956, another big group was freed, including 400 prisoners from Belene and 80 from Varna.

Then came the Hungarian Revolution which quickly turned to a blood bath. The communists feared it might spread to Bulgaria and the other communist countries, so the releases stopped, arrests and trials went on, and the old prison tactics were resumed. The pendulum was swinging back again. Thus the short-lived hope for better conditions died amongst the blood and death of the Hungarian Revolution. The cells filled up again.

At the end of August, the political prisoners were gradually removed from Varna. I was in the last group, with 82 others. At the station we were put into two freight trucks. The next evening we got off the train at Stara Zagora, and were taken by truck to the prison there.

I LOSE MY NEW TESTAMENT

At Stara Zagora we were placed in one man cells; six to a cell. It was most unpleasant there because they often had surprise inspections in the middle of the night. This caught us in the middle of Bible study meetings late at night. The guards wore soft cloth shoes and we couldn't hear them coming. Shortly after we arrived, the cell door was opened and we were all taken to the toilet and locked in. When we returned to the cell we found all our bags had been opened and the contents piled in the middle of the floor. Even the mattresses had been ripped open! Everything written or printed was gone, including my Testament!

What a loss, but I was so happy that by this time I had memorized 47 chapters of God's Word. They were hidden in my heart where they could not be taken from me. These 47 chapters were my "Bible."

One day an imprisoned Catholic priest told me there was an old Bible in the library. This was unbelievable! A Bible in a communist library! Evidently the prison officials had no idea it was there. I rushed to the library at the first chance and tried not to look too excited as I took it back to my cell. I kept it for several weeks. All my cell mates began to read it; then the prisoners in the adjacent cells; and soon everyone in the prison block wanted to read it. I passed it through the bars from one cell to another. These men "devoured" the Scriptures. In freedom many had refused to read God's Word. Now, they hungrily read its words of blessings. We circulated the Bible for weeks. It passed through countless hands.

Finally, of course, the news got back to the Prison Director and he exploded with rage! Of course, I was the "religious criminal" of Stara Zagora so I was sent for. He screamed, "Where did you get that Bible, Popov? How did you smuggle it into prison?"

"But," I replied, "I didn't smuggle it in. It was here in your library all the time."

He was struck dumb. He couldn't believe it. I showed him the prison library stamp on the inside cover. I thought he was going to have a heart attack! He ordered me out. On the way out, I couldn't resist a jibe at him and said, "Thank you for the use of your Bible, Comrade."

BIBLE CLASSES IN THE PRISON YARD

It was a constant challenge to me to find new opportunities to minister to the continual change of prisoners. New ones would come in and older men would be taken out to new prisons or to be released. All in all, I had the opportunity at one time or another to minister to several thousand men, one way or another directly or through tapping on prison walls.

I will cite only one example of how I was able to use almost any pretext to preach the Gospel.

Stara Zagora was full of younger prisoners. A new wave of arrests had filled the prison to overflowing. When I arrived there and saw all the new, young faces, I said, "Thank You, Lord, for the new congregation You've sent me." Of course, I wish they had not been arrested, but since they were, I'm glad I was put amongst them.

Unlike most pastors, I changed "churches" not by a vote of the congregation, but by order of a prison commandant. All through the thirteen years, it seemed when I had done my best at one prison, the commander obliged me by ordering me to another prison where I had a new congregation.

Another difference was my congregation couldn't get up and walk out. They were a "captive" audience. I saw humor in this situation and I told the men. They laughed with me and said, "It's fine, pastor, as long as you don't take a collection!"

Laughter was vital to prisoners and I did my best to keep a sense of humor and perspective. The first sign a man was descending into madness was when he stopped laughing. When this happened all the fellow prisoners, who looked on one another as brothers, spent much time trying to lift the man back to normalcy. Without the prison humor, we all would have gone mad.

So in Stara Zogara I found a new congregation of young men recently arrested.

I prayed all night, "God, help me reach these men. Show me how." Since we were under surveillance, I had to find some way to teach them God's Word secretly.

Then the Lord showed me the answer! I spoke fairly good English from my Bible school year in England. So, I went to the commandant and asked for permission to teach the men English.

He replied, "Popov, what are you up to now? I know you. You are interested only in misleading these young men into your foolish religion. Won't you ever learn that your pastor days are over — for good! No, and get out of here!" he shouted.

Then the idea struck me. We had a 90-minute exercise period each day. Why not use that?

So, I passed word to all prisoners who wanted to learn or improve their English to meet me in the corner of the exercise yard the next day. I couldn't wait for the hour to come. When it did, I found myself surrounded by about 30 prisoners, some who spoke a little English. They were very interested in improving their English. For several weeks, I taught them enough English to understand me clearly. Then I started "Phase Two" of my plan.

I started speaking entirely in English about the Bible and God's Word. The prison guards couldn't speak English. So they came up to listen in, shrugged and walked off. If they had known why I was smiling! I was able freely to preach and teach the Gospel to the young men in English. Their hunger to learn better English brought them there each day until the Word of God began to take hold. I learned later the prison commander asked the guards what I was up to and they replied, "Popov's out there teaching English." The commander shrugged, "If that's how he wants to waste his exercise period, it's no concern of mine."

The Bible classes in the exercise yard continued for several weeks. The men drank in God's Word. Not only had the men learned English but a great deal about God's Word and the Word began bearing fruit.

A significant change took place in the lives of several of the men. Several stopped smoking even though they had sworn they never could.

One of the men who couldn't open his mouth without cursing, asked me one day after the Bible Class, "Pastor Popov, what has happened to me, I don't swear any more!"

Several came to me and said they wanted to become Christians. The change in their lives was remarkable and noticed by all the other men.

They began whispering to the other men and the men passed the Gospel from one cell to another. Men sat up at night in the cell talking about the Bible and God.

God became the number one topic in the cells late at night. A warm spirit of brotherhood and love passed from cell to cell.

"Graduates" of my Bible class began conducting Bible classes of their own in the cells at night.

I am not exaggerating when I say that the influence of these Bible classes reached into every cell-block at Stara Zogara. I myself was surprised. I learned a lesson there: God's Word grows and spreads most in a condition of suffering and privation. This is what made the spiritual harvest I was able to reap so abundant in communist prisons.

How my heart rejoiced when I saw the influence of God's Word on the prisoners. Some, of course, had not changed, but many lives were changed and the difference in Stara Zogara was real and noticeable. When the lights went out at night you could almost hear the buzz of men talking about God's Word and what this or that Scripture meant.

Even those who didn't believe were deeply impressed by the change in the lives of several of the men. They could argue against the Bible, but they couldn't refute the changed lives.

Finally, this came to the attention of the prison director and he summoned me. "Popov, I know you've been up to something. Several of the men are praying in their cells and others are going around all day spouting rubbish about God. I know you're behind this somehow. Now, what's going on?" he demanded.

I replied, "Sir, you know I am a pastor. If, as you communists say, I was a spy, I would be teaching the men spy things would I not? But I am a pastor and only a pastor. So I talk about God. Can I help it if the men like to talk about God too? You took me from my pulpit. You can keep me from a Bible, you can imprison me all you like, but you can't take out of my heart my desire to serve my Lord.

"I have done nothing subversive. I have not spoken against any man or communism. I have only spoken of God. As long as I breathe, I will continue to speak about Him. I will only stop when I am dead."

He summoned the guard and shouted, "Take this man out of here!"

I was taken to the punishment cell and kept there on water only for a month. But it was worth it. I spent the month tapping to the two men in the cells on either side of me.

One day at Stara Zogara I was called before a Secret Police official named Tanio. It was the same day that de Gaulle came into power in France. A tall, thin young DS man was also present in Tanio's office, and soon Tanio left me alone with him.

The young DS man and I talked for about two hours. From what he said, I knew that he not only knew all about me but about all the pastors and congregations. Perhaps he had been a believer, or had relatives who were believers. He knew about the life in our churches and was well versed in church history.

He would be very glad to help me, he said; that was why he had come. But since he had been sent by the Secret Police, I didn't expect anything good to come of it.

We began talking about religion, although he was wary when it came to God. He was cordial and agreeable and we became completely taken up with the subject.

After we had talked about the pastors and congregations, he steered the conversation into politics. The most important question of the day to the communists was whether the French would elect Charles de Gaulle as president. The communist newspapers said that his election would be a grave mistake. I didn't know anything about it, but I decided if the communist papers were against it, I was for it.

I have no idea why, but the young man asked me, "Popov, do you believe de Gaulle will take over?"

"I not only believe that he will do it but I believe he has already done it," was my reply.

He almost struck me. It was as if de Gaulle's coming to power depended upon my answer! "Is it God who has revealed this to you?" he asked. I replied that it had nothing to do with God.

"Are you really a spy with connections in France also?" he asked.

"No," I replied, and couldn't help but chuckle. "It was the articles in your own newspaper you forced us to read that revealed it," I said.

He asked me how long I had been in prison. I said I had been in prison for ten years and that I had only a little time left to serve.

"How little?"

"Four years."

"You think that's a little?"

"It is little after I have been in for ten years."

"Has your sentence been shortened?"

"No, not at all up to now."

In fact, my prison term had been shortened by about one year. The principle was that if one worked two days, his term was shortened by one day. But the young man meant a sentence shortened by a pardon.

Then he looked at me sympathetically and said, "We will try to shorten your term."

The alarm bells rang instantly. I had long ago learned two things: beware when the DS offered help and beware when they call you "Comrade."

He answered that all I had to do was become a member of the Cultural Society, give lectures and do what they said.

I answered that I could never do that. "I have already served ten years. I won't compromise my Christian stand. To compromise now, with only a short time left — I never will do it!"

He tried to persuade me, but I insisted that I would not alter my decision. Around and around we went. Finally, exasperated, he expressed his regret that he would not be able to help me. When I returned to my cell, I told my comrades about the conversation. They then said that at exactly four o'clock (when I had been talking to the young DS man) it was announced on the state radio that de Gaulle had become head of the government in France.

The effects of the Hungarian Revolution began to wear off, and gradually conditions in the prison improved. Again the pendulum swung. The number of men per cell was reduced to five, and in 1958 it dropped to four. Four men in a "one-man" cell was luxury to me!

By June of 1959, I had lost all evidence of sciatica pains and volunteered to work in a quarry some miles from the prison. It would allow me to meet another group of prisoners. I was always trying to circulate among the prisoners leaving behind a witness for Christ.

We went by truck to the quarry, taking clothes and other necessities with us, as we were to work and sleep there. The whole quarry was surrounded by barbed wire, but the barracks were immaculate, the food was ample and well cooked and there were fruit trees in the yard.

The work was heavy. Some men bored holes in the rock and did the dynamiting, others broke up the huge rocks and loaded them on the wagons which took them to a machine which ground them into stones of the desired size.

Because I was so weak, I found quarrying very

hard work. We used 22-pound sledge hammers to break up the big rocks. It was difficult for me just to lift the hammer, much less break the rocks. My whole body ached, but I had wonderful opportunities to work for Christ. I started up a Bible Class at the quarry barracks right under their noses, and they never found out about it. Even the ever-present informer evidently didn't report me. I could only conclude that he was enjoying the Bible classes too.

On March 1, 1961, several other prisoners and I were shipped by freight car back to infamous Persin prison. We arrived on Saturday and had to wait in a cold and dirty receiving room until Monday. The food we were given at Stara Zagora had been eaten during the trip, so we went hungry until Monday.

Before we were assigned to work, we were interrogated once again by the Secret Police. When I said I was an evangelical pastor, one of the Secret Police said that the Russians had put Yuri Gagarin in orbit between the earth and the planets and he had not found God anywhere up there. All the other prisoners looked at me, waiting for my reply. I said, "The kind of God Gagarin looked for with his eyes does not exist."

The officer shot back, "Wonderful Popov, I'm so glad to hear you don't believe in God anymore. Maybe prison has done you some good after all."

I replied, "You're wrong, I do believe there is a God. I don't believe in the God you are looking for, but I do believe in a God who is Spirit and Truth and who can never be discovered by rockets."

That made him furious and he ordered me out. As I left I saw the other prisoners smiling quietly.

Along with a group of men, I was ordered to Barracks Number Two on Persin. I hardly recognized the island. The whole island was covered with newly planted trees; good roads had been built on the embankments, and there was a handsome new four-story administration building. We passed the first barracks area. Instead of our old huts there were fine-looking quarters for the prisoners on the high embankments.

But I discovered it was reserved for the criminal prisoners. Religious or political prisoners had no such luck.

At Barracks Number Two I found the old familiar buildings, but the people were new. There were also modern three-story buildings where the soldiers lived. Evidently they planned to use Persin as a prison for a long time to come. The work was quite varied and very hard, but because they needed our labor they fed us one good meal a day. I met some of my old friends back at Persin and they said, "Pastor we're so glad to see you again. We're sorry you're still in prison, but if you have to be in prison we're glad you're back with us!"

I started Bible classes with the Bible being the 47 chapters I had memorized. The work was extremely hard, but late at night, though exhausted, I conducted the classes. Several new men joined our circle and it grew. Once we even had a sympathetic guard who served as our "look-out" while the Bible classes were conducted. If another guard approached, he gave us a warning signal and I would switch to a "normal" conversation.

My main goal now was to train other prisoners to conduct Bible classes on their own.

Over the years I had left Bible classes in every prison, and several in Stara Zagora. But by now I had been imprisoned for nearly 13 years and my heart ached to be back with my family. Now I felt that my prison work was coming to a close. With the time reduced by hard labor from 15 years to 13 years and two months, my time was almost up. To give you an idea of how long 13 years are, when I was kidnaped from my home, my daughter, Rhoda, was a little girl of 9. Now, she was a married woman and had a daughter of her own. (She married a fine Christian medical intern in Sweden.)

My life had a huge hole cut out of it. I could have been released many times if I had agreed to be a puppet pastor, but I could not. Many times I was offered the chance of freedom by the DS if I would "conform" and help in the destruction of Christianity in Bulgaria. There was even talk that I would be made the head of a religious denomination with a fine office and a good salary. I would have had to spy on the members, the pastors, and they would spy on me. At one time I had been battered and starved senseless where I was a human tape recorder in the hands of the DS, but that only increased my resolve that I would die before I would ever willingly yield or compromise.

The Fruits of Imprisonment

I came to the end of my 13-year imprisonment with my faith intact and stronger than ever; with my self-respect firm, for I had never taken the easy way. And I had the great, great joy of knowing that in every prison and every cell block I had been in, I had left behind men who now knew Christ because I was there. I knew that where I had been, Bible classes were being conducted, and the fruit of my ministry remained. On countless cell walls, the Scriptures I had scratched in would be there to bring hope and comfort to the prisoners who followed me.

I knew that men I had never laid eyes on were serving Christ because I had the opportunity of "tapping" the Gospel to them. I don't label myself a hero or martyr, but as I neared my release and looked back I could honestly and truthfully say that it was worth those 13 years of torture, beatings, starvation, suffering and separation from loved ones to be a "pastor" to the thousands of communist prisoners my path had crossed.

The prisoners were as happy for my release as I was. On the evening of September 24, I waited during roll-call to be told to pack my belongings, but it didn't happen. The cell door was locked behind me. After half an hour, the key turned in the lock and the guard came in.

"Haralan Popov," he said, "pack up your things. Tomorrow you are free."

Everyone in the cell jumped up and cheered. I didn't have much to pack. My prison clothes I divided among the poorer prisoners. I had only my wearing apparel. That night I didn't sleep a wink; I just waited for the break of day.

When the door opened next morning I said good-by to my friends. Several I had led to Christ. They gathered around me and one of them said, "Pastor, we will never forget you. Thank you for what you gave to us in prison. Because of you, we have found God here." I could hardly restrain my tears.

The guard took me to the prison gate and soon a wagon drawn by two horses came and drove me to freedom. It was 8 a.m. when we arrived at Headquarters. A thorough search was made of my clothing and my suitcase, then I was issued papers that would serve as my identification card until I had time to get a regular one. I went out into the yard. No one was about except the guard at the gate. I went to him to ask what I should do next. I asked, "May I go out?"

"Yes, you are cleared. You may go," he said, laughing.

I walked past him in a dream, suitcase in hand. Outside the gate not a soul was in sight. After 13 years, a span of time in which my baby girl had become a wife and mother, I was out from behind prison bars. I wasn't really free, for I was still an ex-prisoner and unlicensed evangelical pastor in a communist land, but at least, the walls of the prison were behind me.

I looked at them from the outside and thought of the lonely nights of torture, the beatings I had suffered. I thought of the starvation and the nine months of solitary confinement in the airless pit.

I remembered the flowing Niagara of horrors and the unbroken river of suffering. But I also remembered the men who had found God.

As I stood looking at the prison walls behind me, I thought, *Yes, to leave behind men who know and serve Christ, it was worth it all.* And it truly was. I can honestly say before God it was worth it all.

Little did I realize I was ending a period as a pastor to men in communist prisons and was soon to become an underground pastor to those whose churches had been closed.

I took a firm grip on my suitcase and started walking down the main village street. When I arrived at the station it was 9 a.m. and the train had left at 8. The next train didn't leave until evening.

I couldn't think of staying in Belene so close to the prison all day, so I set out on foot for a station further down the railway line.

I arrived there, tired and dusty just before noon after a three hour walk, and found a train leaving within 30 minutes which passed through my home village. It was a journey that would take only a day, but one which but for the hand of God over 13 years, I would never have lived to make.

It was, for me, no less a miracle-journey than that of the Children of Israel.

As I sat on the train, slowly chugging its way across the green, flat plains of our country, I looked out the window and prayed, *God help me to serve You as faithfully in freedom as I tried to do in prison. Don't let the easier circumstances lessen my dedication.*

I would rather be truly faithful in prison than let the easier life outside weaken my faith. I need not have had any fear. Things were almost as bad outside.

I arrived at the station in my home town of Krasno

Gradiste around 8 p.m. and walked half a mile down the dusty road of the village to a small, thatched-roof house on the edge of town where my uncle and aunt lived.

I knocked on the door. It opened and my aunt took one look at me and cried out, "Haralan, is it really you?" This wasn't just an exclamation of surprise. It was a serious question, for prison had brought such visible changes in me I often was not recognized by old friends.

I had gone into prison a young pastor in the prime of life. I came out broken in health, bowed over and a mere shadow of the man I once was.

My prison years had leaped the gap from relative youth to being a man now physically elderly.

"It is you!" My aunt exclaimed as my uncle came hurrying from the other room to see what the commotion was all about. He hugged me saying, "Haralan, never in all our lives did we expect to see you again." He stood back looking me over, "What has happened to you?"

Then it dawned on me that I must have looked really awful! I had long ago become used to my "new appearance," but my uncle still thought of me as I appeared fourteen years ago when he last saw me. He couldn't disguise the dismay on his face, though he tried.

Poor uncle! He tried so hard to lift my spirits, but I would steal a glance at him and catch him looking at me with sad eyes. The next thing I knew, I was saying, "Uncle, don't worry about me. The worst is over. God has been with me and in many ways it's been worthwhile."

My aunt looked scoldingly at my uncle and said, "Now look at you! You were going to encourage Haralan and it's ended up with you down in the dumps and him having to encourage you!" I couldn't help but laugh.

Two days later there was a knock at the door and

there stood Ladin, my younger brother! He grabbed me and hugged me. Ladin is big and strong, much stronger than he looks, and I was like a matchstick. "Ladin," I said, "take it easy or you'll finish what the prison started!"

"Haralan," he said, with tears of joy brimming in his eyes, "it's so good to see you! So many times I thought you'd never make it." Ladin had good reason for his doubts. After his own five years of imprisonment he brought food to me in prison whenever it was permitted and saw me there. Every time the authorities permitted food to be brought, Ladin was right there. "Good old Ladin," I said, "You stuck by me all the way. Next to the Lord's faithfulness, you helped me make it."

Around dusk, Ladin and I went for a walk down the small tree-lined main street of the village. It gave us a chance to talk. We stopped in an empty park in the middle of the village and sat on the single, unpainted park bench. Ladin told me how, after his five years' imprisonment, he was now barred from his pulpit for life. He explained how he had been ministering as an "underground pastor" and of the many times he had been arrested and beaten for his work since his release from prison. I had led Ladin to Christ myself when he was on the verge of committing suicide many years before. Now, hearing of his own torture and present ordeal I asked, "Ladin, in all those years in prison, did you ever resent me for leading you to the Lord since that led to your torture?"

"No," he replied, "Never. Not for one moment!" And from the firm tone of his voice I knew he really meant it.

From what Ladin told me as we sat there, it appeared that in my 13 years absence, the entire country had become one vast "prison"; that I had just passed from a smaller prison into a larger prison.

"Haralan," Ladin said quietly, "things are very, very bad for all the believers. A great change has taken place in Bulgaria. Many country churches have been closed and the city churches are controlled by the communists, with their own men in the pulpits and the Secret Police in every meeting. But there is a large body of believers who haven't bowed their knee to Baal yet and we'll never give in. We're meeting in barns and homes and any place else we can meet."

"Ladin," I replied, "it sounds just like what I did in prison these 13 years. It looks like I'll be able to put that experience to good use now."

We sat silently on the park bench, each lost in his own thoughts, watching the squirrels playing on the ground while the evening wind grew chilly. We said little as we made our way back to our uncle's house, each deep in his own thoughts.

As we walked along, the evening wind had now become quite cold. A storm was building up in the North and it seemed an ominous portent of things to come.

* * *

But God's hand was also upon us. He had been with me through conditions which stagger the imagination and He would still be with me.

The first "miracle" after my release was when I was given a "Resident's Permit" for Sofia, our capital city, and received police permission to go there to get my identification card.

I don't know how I got it. To have a "Resident's Permit" to live in Sofia today means what Roman citizenship meant to Paul. Sofia was the heart of everything and many Bulgarians would have given much money to get such a permit but couldn't. For in Bulgaria, Russia and other communist lands, the communists try to control every movement of the people.

You must have an "Internal Passport" even to move about the country. You don't just pick where you want to live. You live *where* the communists say and you move *when* they say.

So never in a million years could I have arranged a resident's permit for Sofia. But God arranged it, using the communist officials to do it. He still had a plan for my life.

I said, "Thank You, Lord, I know You've got work for me to do in Sofia," and went on my way there hoping to find a small place to live.

But I was both an "ex-prisoner" and an "unregistered" evangelical pastor. Being just one of those things was enough to put the "mark of Cain" on a man for life. And I was both! As soon as the housing authorities saw from my papers what I was, I was sent away.

I looked everywhere on my own but couldn't find a place to live — not even a small room, much less an apartment. Some of my former church members risked trouble by inviting me to live with them for a while. But not wanting to cause them danger, I kept looking. I prayed, "God, even the sparrows have a nest. I know You have a place for me somewhere."

And He did. I soon found a deserted, empty half-attic which was used to store trunks and suitcases. It was tiny, dusty and filled with cobwebs. The rain leaked right through the roof. It had no heating or water and was so tiny I had room only for a small bed, a tiny desk and a chair. The Christians who saw it were surprised that I was able to live in such a little nook, but I was happy with it. I told one of my former church members, "In prison I lived for years in a space as small as this with 7 or 8 others."

I could tell from his doubtful expression, he was having a hard time believing me. It was *so tiny*.

To get to my tiny half-attic, I climbed five flights of stairs to the top floor of the building, then climbed a ladder through a hole in the ceiling and lifted myself into the attic. It was quite a job getting even a tiny bed upstairs!

When it rained, the rain dripped through holes in the roof and because my small bed itself covered most

133 •

of the tiny room, the water dripped mostly on the bed. A single window pane was broken out making it very cold. But when I taped it with paper, the light was cut off, so I decided I would rather be cold than be in darkness, so I left it broken out and spent the winter days huddled up with blankets around me. But the room was a gift from God and I thanked Him for it.

The first night that I spent in my cold attic room was stormy, and rain dripped all over my bed. I lay huddled in the blankets given me by Christians, thinking of Ruth, Rhoda and Paul in Sweden and what they were doing that night. *Would I ever see them again,* I wondered. At last I drifted off into a fitful, troubled sleep.

AMAZING OLD "BABBA" MARIA

There was only one consolation to my attic "home." That was "Babba" Maria. "Babba" is our affectionate Bulgarian name for "Grandma" and "Babba" Maria was a very wrinkled, but vital, energetic 72-year-old Christian lady who lived on a lower floor. She became like a "mother hen" to me.

Babba Maria was a remarkable old lady and one of the most unforgettable people I've ever met. She was an irrepressible "take charge" woman who seemed to really believe that her heavenly Father owned the cattle on a thousand hills.

She had been a Christian worker since her youth and had an irrepressible, contagious, overflowing faith in God that uplifted everyone around her. What a spiritual giant and pillar of strength Babba Maria was! Nothing ever seemed to get her down. When things looked blackest, you could count on old Babba Maria to grin and say, "Now, who's on the Throne? God, or the devil?" And everyone's spirits would pick up. She was a woman who walked closely with the Lord and who had an unconquerable faith. No one who knew her will ever forget her, especially the communists who once or twice tried to stop one of her prayer meetings.

"Now look here, young man," she sternly lectured a young policeman one day, "God told me to pray. Now who should I obey, you or God?" The young policeman just stammered something and walked off. She was never bothered again.

"Haralan," she said one day, "you get right down out of that attic. We're going to start a prayer meeting and you're going to lead it!"

No one ever dared say "no" to Babba Maria, so I started prayer meetings and Bible classes in her small apartment. I quoted Scriptures from the 47 chapters I had memorized in prison and ministered the Word of God to them and in many ways it was similar to my secret ministry in prison. When I had finished Babba Maria said, "Thank God! We don't have any Bibles, but God has given us a 'Bible' living up in that attic."

From that night on, we met, prayed and I quoted the Scriptures. It was blissful, sweet fellowship. There is nothing sweeter than the fellowship of true believers with one another, when surrounded by difficulty and suffering. I realize now the fellowship Paul missed so much when he wrote to the believers from his prison in Rome.

Soon after the meetings started I received a great gift from God. The news came that Ruth had been able to join a Swedish tourist group coming to Bulgaria and would be on her way to see me soon! How my heart jumped at that news! I had seen Ruth the last time eleven years ago in prison. Babba Maria was as happy as I was and said, "See, Haralan! I told you everything was possible with God."

As the day of Ruth's arrival neared, I was as happy as a child. I couldn't sleep at night and lay in my attic bed, the rain dripping down from the leaky roof, and thought about the last time I had seen Ruth eleven years ago. In those eleven years I had never allowed myself the luxury of thinking of seeing her or the children again. Such hopes had driven strong men mad. But as Babba Maria kept saying, "God is still on the Throne."

The great day finally came. Five hours before Ruth's plane was due, I was at the airport anxiously waiting. The plane was an hour and 14 minutes late and that was the longest hour and 14 minutes I've ever spent. It seemed like 114 years! Finally the flight arrived and I met Ruth just outside the customs hall. "Ruth," I shouted, "over here."

"Haralan," she called back. Soon we were in each other's arms. Eleven long years of no hope of ever seeing her again and here she was! "Haralan!" she gasped, and then choked back the words. I guess I still looked a sight.

We returned to Babba Maria's and she fixed tea for us as Ruth told me of Paul and Rhoda and her husband. My heart was so big I couldn't contain it as I heard of Paul's good grades in school and how little Rhoda was now grown up and had married a fine Christian doctor. Ruth showed me the latest pictures of the children and I laughed and cried at almost the same time.

"Haralan," Ruth said "I'm with the tourist group now. It's the only way I could get into the country and I've got to go back with them soon, but as soon as Paul graduates, gets a job and is able to care for himself I'm coming back here to be with you."

"Ruth, this is no life for you," I replied. "I don't know what the future holds for me, but I don't want to see you living under these conditions. It's better you stay in Sweden. My future is too uncertain."

"Haralan, you're my husband," she tearfully replied, "and I want to be with you wherever you are. I don't care what it's like or how the conditions are."

The day of Ruth's return to Sweden came all too soon and I took her on the sad journey to the airport. We had a tearful farewell, never knowing if we would see each other again. She flew off to Sweden and I returned to my attic room alone, in deep sadness with my heart breaking.

"God," I prayed as I fell on the bed, "give me strength. All my life, I have tried only to do Your will. You didn't fail me in prison. Give me strength now."

In the depth of despair as I cried out from my heart, I felt the presence of God fill my room as I had in the prison cells throughout 13 years. I prayed, "Lord, my life is here with my people." I then fell into a deep sleep.

CHURCH SPIES SPYING ON SPIES

With the excitement of Ruth's visit over I plunged into the secret prayer meetings and Bible study groups in earnest. Gradually the enormity of the tragedy that had overwhelmed our churches in my 13 years absence hit me full force. Everything that Ladin told me was true — and more.

My heart broke as I saw what had happened. Churches that had had 200 or 300 members were now down to 15 or 16! Where once the church had four, five or more meetings a week, now there was only one. Pastors who refused to "cooperate" in the strangulation of the church from within were removed and "cooperative" pastors were put in their places.

Sunday schools were forbidden and DS spies were in every meeting. They wanted to know: who was there, what was said, who prayed too fervently, was there any attempt to "proselyte" new converts?

They needn't have worried because, by and large, the "new pastors" they had installed were over-zealous in enforcing the religious laws.

A police apparatus of total control had reached its octopus-like tentacles around the churches in a deadly embrace.

To make sure of total control of all that was said and done in the churches, the DS had spies in every

137 •

church meeting to spy on their own approved "new pastors." Spies were spying on the spies! Still, many true Christians remained in such churches to keep some sort of witness alive. Among these Christians, there was a joke going around that the DS spies were the most faithful church members of all. They never missed a meeting!

The DS spy in each church tried to keep his identity secret, but the true believers soon found out. The believers asked themselves two questions: who was at almost every meeting? and who seemed to listen most attentively to every empty, dead word spoken by the communist-installed new pastors? Whoever fitted that description best usually turned out to be the DS spy!

In one church, the believers decided the DS man needed the true Gospel. They began to stop him at the door of the church after each sermon, discussing how wonderful the "sermon" was, considerably improving it in the re-telling. The DS spy had to seem very interested to keep up his "front." Meeting after meeting, they met him and talked to him about God until he had enough of these "religious fanatics" and requested a transfer.

But, of course, another "new convert" joined the church shortly and the Christians knew he was the DS replacement. They started on him too. Those irrepressible Christians of that particular church drove one DS man after another to request a transfer!

But the communists' "wearing down" tactics were beginning to tell. The technique used was simple. As soon as the "pastor" could *reduce* the number of believers in the church, the authorities stepped in and declared there was "not enough interest" and ordered the church closed and the building put to "more profitable use." The churches in the countryside, towns and villages were especially hard hit, with many closed. Using this clever DS tactic, it never looked like outside persecution. The authorities could always boast "the church was closed for lack of interest."

In each major city, one or two churches were left open but were also "pastored" by men approved by the DS. Foreigners were brought there and shown "freedom of religion" at work. Still a faithful "remnant" remained in even the official churches, determined to maintain their witness and keep the church doors open, so the authorities couldn't say there was "no interest."

Then a new blow hit the believers remaining in the churches. The young men, one by one, began getting summonses to report to the local DS headquarters. There they would be asked, "Why haven't you taken the hint and left the church? There's no place for you there. We want you out and if you don't take the hint, we'll find a way to make ourselves better understood."

Most of the young men refused to give up. One by one, they were ordered back to the DS office at night where they were beaten in such a way that no visible marks would show. The beatings lasted until 5 or 6 a.m., then the men were sent home saying, "If you tell one person, even your wife, what has happened it will mean your life. Be back here at 10 again tonight!"

Many of our finest young Christians had to leave their families each night after dinner to report for the nightly beatings.

They suffered in silence for Christ, telling no one.

These secret, night-time beatings of anyone who seemed to be "zealous" in their faith in Christ were a regular night-time ordeal for many of our people — just as they are today in Russia, Bulgaria and many other communist lands.

"Officially" it doesn't happen but thousands of men today are silently carrying this burden for Christ.

UNDERGROUND WITH GOD

Faced with the closed or communist-controlled

churches, we followed the pattern of the Early Church in Rome in creating a "catacomb" or "Underground Church."

In the larger cities the Christians began forming underground groups meeting and worshiping in believer's homes scattered around the city, always changing the meeting place to avoid discovery.

Such meetings are dangerous because in all communist lands, it's illegal to have any religious service outside the four walls of a "licensed" church. The underground churches desperately needed Bible teaching and the same full range of pastoral help as any "normal" church. So I dedicated my years to the Underground Church and became very active going to other believers' houses throughout Sofia conducting underground meetings, prayer sessions and Bible classes. My schedule was full of such meetings.

A "pattern" of my underground meetings soon began to emerge. A meeting would be called in a Christian's home for around midnight. The two favorite hours were midnight and around 6 p.m. For midnight meetings people started "drifting" in by twos and threes around 8 p.m., a full four hours before the meeting was due to begin. Never more than 3 or 4 came at a time so as not to arouse attention. A few minutes after the arrival of the first two or three, two or three more would "drop in." A few more minutes would pass and the next two or three would come. In this way a sizable group could gather without attracting attention. I was usually the last to arrive as I often hurried from one underground group to another and couldn't afford the long waiting period before the meeting began. By midnight, on arrival at the believer's house I almost always found the streets deserted and the neighborhood in absolute stillness. All shutters were closed and locked. You wouldn't think a person was around, but entering I often found twenty-five to thirty people packed and jammed inside waiting for the meeting to start.

People usually make noise. Even if they don't talk or say a word there is usually some kind of noise from people just *being there* — a cough, a shuffle or something. But I had noticed in prison and now again that Christians worshiping underground often make no noise at all, even in groups of twenty-five or more. It is a strange sight.

The men usually stood along the walls. The women sat on beds or makeshift chairs, and the younger people squatted on the floor. Sometimes, we took the risk of singing a hymn (we sang very softly to keep from being overheard). Tears would flow as we met and sang the beautiful songs of the Church just as the believers of the Early Church.

"My dear brothers and sisters in Christ," I would begin. "We meet here to worship our Lord and hear His Word. He is here with us this night." On and on I would continue. It was dangerous to meet, so when we did meet, the meetings lasted up to 3 or 4 hours, ending in prayer for one another and all the other fellow-Christians over our land and in Russia meeting tonight as we were.

With the meeting finally over, we had to leave the same way we came, by two and threes. Again, I would be the first to leave due to my heavy schedule. It took as long to disperse as it did to gather. After well-attended meetings Christians would still be leaving at 6 or 7 o'clock in the morning as people were filling the street to go to work.

Such small underground churches were springing up all over the country as the persecution drove the believers to this depth of sincerity and dedication, willing to risk their homes, their jobs and even their freedom to assemble and worship together.

"BIRTHDAY EVANGELISM"

We always improvised and found new ways to meet, teach the Word of God and fellowship together. I soon discovered that one of the best times to have meetings was on birthdays because it was common and safe for groups to get together on birthdays. There was no danger of discovery and no need to gather secretly or sing in hushed voices. After all, it was only a "birthday party." Birthdays soon became one of the favorite occasions for the underground churches to meet and worship together.

Birthdays gave such a wonderful opportunity that many Christian families with three or four members in the family began having *fifteen or twenty "birthdays" a year!* I myself had so many "birthdays" that if I were as many years old as I had birthdays, I'd be almost Methuselah's age! We had the "oldest" Christians in the world in the underground churches.

Weddings and funerals also provided wonderful opportunities for us to openly preach the Gospel. One day the wedding ceremony, at which I could not officiate since I was an "unregistered" pastor, took about ten minutes. Afterward someone said, "All right, Pastor Popov, come on up and wish the bride and groom happiness." I went up to the front of the room and "wished them happiness" for three hours! I preached, quoted from God's Word and taught the Scriptures just as if I were back in my pulpit before my arrest.

What wonderful times these weddings were!

After one wedding I had preached an unusually long time, and everyone sat listening to every word. Afterward one of the men came up and said, "Haralan, I'll bet you're always praying someone will hurry up and get married just so you can have a meeting." His daughter, about 16, was standing beside him. I told her, "Now, Larissa, I'm counting on your wedding next year. Don't let me down." She blushed as her father laughed.

In countless ways we improvised and found new ways of meeting, worshiping and spreading the Gospel underground. The Lord was wonderfully with me many times. Once as I taught a group of believers at mid night in a home, we heard footsteps coming down the sidewalk and stopping just outside the door. One of the men looked through the shutters and whispered, "It's a policeman." We began to pray fervently in our hearts. Soon we could hear him walking away.

Of course, sometimes the secret police managed to discover a secret meeting and the leader was arrested, the names of those attending were taken down and the men summoned to the police station headquarters for interrogation and sometimes for all night "instruction sessions" of beatings in the DS basement.

But a beautiful thing began to happen in the Underground Church. As the fires of persecution grew, they burned away the chaff and stubble and left only the golden wheat. The suffering *purified* the Church and united the believers in a wonderful spirit of brotherly love such as must have existed in the Early Church. Petty differences were put aside. Brethren loved and cared for one another and carried one another's burdens. There were no nominal or "lukewarm" believers. It made no sense to be a half-hearted Christian when the price for faith was so great. There came a great spiritual depth and richness in Christ I have never seen in the times before when we were free.

It was as if the spirit of the Early Church had descended in all its beauty, fullness and love upon the believers of the Underground Church. Every man, woman and youth was forced to "count the cost" and decide if serving Christ was worth the suffering. And to the communists' great regret, this was the healthiest thing they could have done for the Church, for the insincere gave up but the true Christians became aware of what Christ meant to them and became more dedicated than ever before.

When believers were discovered meeting secretly, some were sent off in exile to remote parts of our country. On arrival they began to spread the Word of God there as they had back home, just as the disciples of the Early Church, driven by persecution, spread the Word of God to the far corners of the then known world.

Christian history has come "full circle" in the Underground Church in communist lands today.

THE BIBLE SCAVENGER

Working now in the Underground Church, I began to face the tragedies of Christians without the Word of God.

No one can begin to describe in words the empty void in the heart of a Christian denied God's Word. Nothing could be more "unnatural." It is like a fish without water, or a bird without air. Christians are *creatures of God's Word* and must have that Word to grow spiritually.

One day on the street, I met an old man in very dirty clothes, who approached me saying, "Pastor, you don't know me, but I know you and I have something here I want to show you." I was a little suspicious of him, thinking he might be with the DS. But then I decided none of the proud men in the Secret Police would have appeared this dirty, so he must be for real. He pulled open his tattered coat and showed me a ragged, partly burned book in terrible condition. It was so soiled and dirty, I couldn't even tell at first what kind of book it was. He then flipped open the pages and I saw that it was a Bible! It was partly burned and had sections missing — but it was a Bible!

Taking him by the arm and leading him off to the side so we wouldn't be overheard, I asked, "Where did you get this?"

"At the Sofia trash dump," he replied.

"At the trash dump!" I exclaimed.

"How . . . ?" But before I could finish the question he interrupted, "I dig around trash dumps for anything of value and sell it. That's how I make my living. One day I was poking under a pile of rubbish and I saw an old partly-burned book. I picked it up and found it was a half-burned Bible. It dawned on me that this must be one of the Bibles they are taking away from the people and destroying. I decided I must have found where they were dumping the Bibles and I figured if that's where they burned and destroyed them, that's where I would go to get them back."

He went on, "Since then, I've been going out there because they know me there. But now, I get only enough other junk to be a "cover" for my real purpose of getting Bibles. I'm only after the Bibles from now on and getting them back in circulation. I figure if the authorities don't want them around, they must be good."

I couldn't help but laugh inside. This kind of humor was so typical of people living under communism. "And besides," he went on, "I can make a living stealing these Bibles back from the ones who stole them in the first place.

"Here Pastor," he whispered, handing me the Bible. "I want you to have this for your work." I started to thank him as he turned to walk away.

"Where are you going?" I asked. "I want to thank you some way."

"No," he replied, "I've got to be going."

I knew where he was going. I never saw him again, but from time to time, I saw partly burned or very soiled parts of Bibles in the underground meetings and I knew the old "Bible scavenger" was still at work.

How just! The communists stole the Bibles from the people. He stole them from the communists and got the Bibles back into circulation!

I preached and taught the Word of God in the many small underground churches which were now meeting regularly around Sofia. The Bible meant so much to me, because I only knew 47 chapters by heart and missed the others.

After a late night meeting with an underground group of believers, a young girl about sixteen years old came up to me. I recognized her as a new Christian who had just recently joined this Underground Church.

"Pastor Popov," she said, looking at the partly burned Bible the old man had given me, "could I borrow your Bible until tomorrow morning?"

"Well, yes certainly," I replied.

She took the Bible and, sure enough, the next morning she brought it back to me at Babba Maria's. She thanked me and just before leaving turned and asked, "Pastor, could I borrow it again after the meeting tonight?"

"Of course," I said, curious about why she wanted it overnight. The next morning, she again returned it promptly, thanked me and asked, "Where will you be speaking tonight?"

I told her and she replied, "If I come there tonight, can I borrow it again and return it early tomorrow morning?"

I was dying of curiosity and couldn't stand it any longer. "Yes, of course you can, but why? What are you doing with it? Are you sitting up all night reading it?"

"No, Pastor," she replied, "if I take it home and just read it, it will be gone tomorrow morning. I take it home and copy as many verses as I can by hand from midnight to dawn. If I have a good night, I can get several whole chapters done!" she said excitedly.

"One day," she said beaming with pride, "if I keep it up, I'll have a Bible of my own! Won't that be wonderful, Pastor?"

I was deeply touched, and told her, "You can have it tonight and *every night* and during the day too if you want until you get your Bible done." She clasped her hands together, almost jumping for excitement, "Oh, Pastor, thank you!"

After she left, my heart was broken. Here was a

little girl so excited over the prospects of working countless nights, all night long, copying the Scriptures so one day she would have her own Bible. How hungry and desperate my people were for God's Word! This was happening all over Bulgaria. And what about those who didn't have even a partly-burned Bible to copy? It is a great tragedy of our times.

UNDERGROUND "BIBLE FACTORY"

One day I heard about an underground "Bible factory" set up in the back room of a Christian's home just outside Sofia, and made my way out there. Passing through a small rear door so low I had to stoop down, I entered a well-lit room, with heavy drapes carefully placed over the windows. Inside I found a long table and seven people sitting around it hard at work. Most were young people, with an elderly man busily copying away down at the end of the table. They didn't even look up as I was led into the room. I had walked into an underground "Bible factory."

It was an incredible sight which so well shows the plight of Christians in communist lands without Scriptures.

They had somehow secured a Bible and carefully cut it apart in books. Each "work station" at the table was assigned to copy that one book over and over again, by slow, painstaking, hand-lettering. At other "work stations," others were busy with other books such as John, Luke, and Acts. When one group was tired, they were relieved by others in relays so the work wouldn't stop. The hand copying continued 12 hours a day. When a book of the Bible was finished, it was put together with the other books, and stitched into a complete Bible.

When the completed, hand-lettered Bible was carefully bound in leather, it was speeded on its way to a group of Christians in an Underground Church somewhere in Bulgaria. This "Bible factory" produced

25 hand-written Bibles a year — always at great risk and incredibly long hours of labor.

Though I never saw them, I heard of other such "Bible factories" as our fellow Christians of the Underground Church desperately worked to produce Scriptures for the Bible-starved people.

One evening I had finished a meeting of an underground Bible class in a believer's home when one of the Christians handed me a piece of cardboard with typed pages inside, saying, "Look at this, Pastor." I examined it and it was a gospel book entitled *Calvary's Road* by Roy Hession. But it was a completely typewritten book, with the typed pages bound in by needle and thread between cardboard covers.

I asked, "Where did you get this? This is wonderful!"

He explained, "There's a crippled man who speaks English living on the other side of town. He has an ancient, broken-down typewriter. He gets these Bible-teaching books and since he's crippled, he spends all his time translating and typing them out a few carbon copies at a time. As soon as he's finished, he starts typing the whole book all over again. He makes 4 to 5 carbon copies each time he retypes it all. His typed books are being circulated from hand to hand all over Bulgaria."

I secured his address and went over to his tiny apartment. As I entered the first thing I saw were stacks of paper piled high all over his apartment. I couldn't believe it. To buy such a quantity of paper would immediately attract the attention of the Secret Police who would start asking questions. He saw the astonishment on my face and laughed, answering my question even before I could ask it, "Pastor, where there's a will, there's a way. I have Christians all over Sofia going out for me, each one buying a little paper here and a little there in small quantities. They all bring it here and I use it to type out these books I've translated."

On and on he went, explaining how he worked as he showed me one book after another in the process of translation. Then he showed me a stack of finished books ready to go. His little apartment was a veritable underground Christian bookstore right here in the capital of communist Bulgaria!

Though he couldn't get out of the apartment, the books and literature he produced on his old typewriter in this tiny crowded apartment in Sofia were bringing countless blessings to hundreds and possibly thousands all across Bulgaria.

Such heroic efforts of the Underground Church touched me deeply. I saw sacrifice beyond measure but even such heroic sacrifice and efforts as these *couldn't begin* to meet the need of our people for Bibles, hymn books, gospels and literature for our youth. All these heroic efforts produced only a mere trickle of what was needed.

The "Bible factories" worked day and night, but at most produced only 25 to 30 Bibles a year.

Young Christians, such as the young girl, borrowed any Bible available and desperately copied them all night long but this was not enough. One old typewriter in the hands of a crippled man produced some books but it was only a drop in the bucket compared to the need.

Again and again, young Christians approached me saying, "Pastor, we need a Bible. Isn't there one somewhere for us?"

My heart broke seeing the need of the underground churches. All across the land, tragedy was stalking the Underground Church. My heart wept as I saw young Christians begging for the use of a Bible for just a few hours.

And what about the coming generation? We couldn't possibly teach them God's Word *without* God's Word. We saw youth carrying beautiful, full color books on atheism — and we had *nothing* to give them. I lay in my attic room praying, deeply distressed. Something had to be done. We could never meet the need among ourselves by hand-copying Bibles. It was clear someone had to get help from the outside.

It became more and more apparent that we had to have help from our fellow-Christians outside the Iron Curtain. Someone had to get out to the Free World and awaken our fellow-Christians to the need and somehow get Bibles in. Someone had to speak for the Underground Churches which had no voice. Several of the people urged that I must be the one. "After all," they pointed out, "you have a family in Sweden and have the best apparent 'reason' for asking to be permitted to leave Bulgaria." And, of course, I did long to be united with my family.

My Urgent Mission

It was heartbreaking to think about leaving my country and the believers there, many of whom I had personally led to the Lord and to whom I had been both spiritual father and pastor.

In my mind I had prepared myself to stay with my people. But many of them kept urging me to go, recognizing that only by making our needs known could we ever get the help we needed. Outwardly, they stressed, it would appear to the authorities that I wanted only to join my family which was perfectly natural. Secretly, my real and most important mission would be to get help for the Underground Church — a mission far more important than family desires.

Instead of having Ruth return here as planned, I now knew by all means I must get out to the Free World. Babba Maria and Christians across Bulgaria began to pray that God would open the doors and I would be able to undertake this mission. Prayer meetings were held all over Bulgaria. I got word to Ruth asking her to write letters to the Swedish government to put pressure on the Bulgarian authorities, asking approval for me to come there. I applied for permision to leave and was immediately turned down. Still the Christians prayed.

One day I received a letter from the Minister of Internal Affairs ordering me to report to their office. Going out the door Babba Maria stopped me and said, "Brother Haralan, it's your passport. You're going to get permission to go!"

When I arrived at the office, I was brusquely ordered into the office of the Chief Deputy — the second highest official of that department. He was a large, fat man with hard, determined features, not a man to be toyed with. As I entered and sat down, he sat staring at me. I could tell he was very angry. His hands were almost shaking with barely concealed wrath. Suddenly he shouted, "Popov, your daughter in Sweden has written to the Russian Premier asking for your release!"

I couldn't believe my ears.

The Russian Premier!

Rhoda was really going to the top! The letter had been sent here to Sofia and was on the desk before me. The Chief Deputy picked it up and waved it at me. "Do you think this is going to help your case?" he shouted. "If you do you're sadly mistaken." With his face flushed red with anger, the Chief Deputy pointed his finger at me and said, "Popov, you are to write your family, telling them never to write another letter on your behalf. You must never make out another application to leave!"

With his voice rising in anger, he shouted, "I am warning you for the last time, Popov. I am in charge of these matters and I will never give you a passport. *You'll leave over my dead body!* You're both an ex-prisoner *and* an unregistered pastor. Just being one of those things would forever bar you from leaving. But you are *both!* Now get out of here and don't ever come back." I almost staggered out the door. I was crushed. All hope seemed gone. Who would speak for the underground churches? Who would tell our story to awaken the sleeping Christians in the Free World?

Next to these questions, the question of never seeing my family again palled into insignificance. It was purely personal. I had a message from the Underground Church to the free world. How could I ever fulfill it now when the Chief Deputy himself stood in the way? Walking back to my attic room, I was deep in despair, "God," I cried out in my heart, "What will happen now to our youth who are asking for Scriptures? To our people who don't have the Bible? Where will help come from?"

When I reached home, I found Babba Maria and two women waiting for me to return with the good news. My mission was vital to all the Christians of the Underground Church, and they were all praying! They knew what was at stake. I told Babba Maria and the others what had happened; how I had been turned down once and for all by the Chief Deputy himself who had sworn I would leave over his dead body.

"Ha!" Babba Maria laughed, "I don't care one bit what he said. It is vital that you go." She went on, "God has told me you are going and it will be very soon. No one can stand in the way of God."

That left me speechless. On one hand I was deeply distressed, but on the other hand Babba Maria was a deeply spiritual woman. I climbed the stairs to my attic room still depressed, but behind me Babba Maria yelled up after me, "Now get your bags packed, Haralan. You're going to Sweden!" Old Babba didn't doubt God for a moment! So typical of the irrepressible faith of Christian women behind the Iron Curtain! She kept on praying for God to do the impossible and open the doors for me to leave.

Then the miracle she prayed for happened.

Just a short time later the Bulgarian Communist Party held its annual conference. Quite unexpectedly a great argument broke out among the "comrades" and the heads began to roll. Several top and middle-level communist officials were booted out, including the Minister for Internal Affairs — and along with him the *very Chief Deputy* who swore to me he would never allow me to go!

Now, just a few days after those threats, *he was out of office himself!* Little did he know that it was little old Babba Maria who "prayed him out of a job"! When I heard the news, I rushed to tell Babba Maria, "Babba, he doesn't know it but he's probably the first high communist official ever prayed out of office!" She just grinned and said, "Well, he may not be the last one either."

He was sure I would never leave, but he hadn't counted on God's plan. No one can stand in God's way.

On December 28, a letter came for me saying, "You are asked to report to the Passport office. Your passport to travel to Sweden to join your family is being granted." How we praised God! *The miracle had happened.*

Babba Maria just smiled and said, "Haralan, I don't like to tell you I told you so, *but I told you so!* God never fails. Now go get your passport!"

It is absolutely unheard of that any former prisoner would be released, much less a prisoner who was also an "outlawed" evangelical pastor. It's absolutely unprecedented in our own country or in Russia. But God had an urgent mission for me in the Free World, and when God has spoken *no one* can interfere. When a chief communist official personally swore I would never leave, God removed him.

Christians all over Bulgaria fasted and prayed for this miracle — and it happened.

Old Babba Maria's words were fulfilled.

I went to the Ministry of Internal Affairs and showed the letter to a clerk. She told me to go to the National Bank and pay a small fee, and to report back with the receipt and get my passport. Ten minutes later I was in the National Bank. Everything I had to do was arranged for promptly — I didn't even have to stand in line for hours. God took care of all the details.

On the following day, the Saturday before New Year's, I received my passport. Next, I received my visa from the Swedish Consul, then took my passport back to the Passport office to get final clearance to travel abroad. I told them that a flight was leaving on Monday, December 31st, for Sweden, and I was advised to come back on Sunday at 11 a.m. to get my passport. Since December 31st was New Year's eve and a holiday, people worked on Sunday to make up for it. Here, too, I saw God's hand, enabling me to leave promptly. Otherwise, I would have had to wait ten days for the next flight to Sweden and who knows who would have seen the documents showing Haralan Popov the "unreformed" evangelical pastor and ex-prisoner was being released? It violated every rule the communists had!

I returned to the passport office at nine on the Sunday morning. At eleven, they began handing out passports to those waiting, but mine was not among them. When I inquired I was told, "We are just giving out the passports to communist countries now. You must wait." Noon came. I thought to myself. *Have the Secret Police changed their minds?*

At 12:30 a man's voice called out, "Haralan Popov." I got up to go over praying, "Lord, Thy will be done."

"Haralan Popov, step over here," the voice called again, "we have your passport ready." I got it and hurried to the Balkan Travel Bureau to get my ticket for the plane next day. Exactly at closing time, at 1 p.m., everything was cleared — passport, visa, and ticket were all in my hand.

God had made the impossible possible for He had an urgent mission for me in the free world. All over the country the underground churches received word that "Pastor Popov is getting out." Their prayers had been answered. There was great rejoicing.

At 8:00 a.m. Monday, December 31, 1962, I was at the airport and the plane left at 10:00 a.m.

After leaving Sofia, we flew to Prague, then over East Germany, touching down in East Berlin for half an hour. I left the plane, but with communist guards around, I felt prison walls still surrounded me there. Back on the plane I asked the stewardess to tell me when we flew over the border from East to West Germany. When we were over the border, I lifted up a prayer of thanks to God that now I was really outside prison walls.

Ten minutes before the ringing in of the New Year, the plane touched down at Arlanda Airport in Stockholm. I have no words to describe the reunion that followed. Ruth, Rhoda, Paul and my son-in-law, John, and little grandson were there. Four days before I had not known whether I would ever see my family again in this life. Every long-standing communist rule had been broken and a Chief Deputy of the communist party had sworn I would leave over his dead body, was suddenly out of office. Now I was here! Tears of joy flowed freely. As I embraced Ruth I thought, *Is this true, or is it a dream?*

It was true. I embraced Rhoda — Rhoda, the little weeping girl I had last seen nearly 15 years ago crying, "Daddy, Daddy," as I was led away. Paul who was only 4 when I was arrested was now almost a man and all these years he had had no father. I tearfully clutched him. What a day of reunion it was!

As we rode home from the airport in the bus, church bells were ringing out the old year and ringing in the new. Hearing them, reminded me of the church bells that Christmas Eve at Persin when I was half-drowned and lying in the frozen mud exhausted and waiting for death. They reminded me of the 13 Christmases I had spent in prison cells, cold and lonely. For me and my family was truly a New Year and a new life.

But that new life has a mission: to speak for the underground churches I left behind the Iron Curtain.

So after a short period of recuperation and being with the children, I told Ruth, "Honey, the time has come for me to do what I came to do. The Christians are counting on me. I must not let them down."

Ruth understood. She always has.

Since then, I have been often away from home and my family on a mission for my *other family* — the faithful Underground Church which is struggling with empty hands to serve Christ in Communist lands.

A Message From the Underground Church

My mission among you in the Free World is to awaken the conscience of the Christians in the Free World to the suffering and needs of our fellow-Christians behind the Iron Curtain. They are today suffering for the faith just as did Peter and Paul and the Christians of the Early Church.

Whether in Bulgaria or Russia or America, we are all part of the *same* Body of Christ. We are all brothers and sisters in Christ, children of the same God. Yet that part of the Body of Christ in the Communist world is being tortured, imprisoned and suffering as never before since the days of the martyrs of the Early Church. Can you not feel their pain?

Recently, several of the leaders of the Underground Church in Russia have reportedly died in prison, including Rev. Bondorenko, a man often called "Russia's Billy Graham" because of his work for Christ.

These courageous Christian leaders were not sentenced to death. According to the Secret Police, they died of "natural causes" — all within a few days of each other. I, myself, have seen hundreds of such "natural" deaths in prison due to the effects of beatings, torture and starvation.

Many thousands are now imprisoned for their faith in Russia, Bulgaria, China and other Communist lands. Behind a carefully contrived image of religious freedom, the roll of Christian martyrs of our day grows tragically longer. Behind the current propaganda of Bibles being printed in Communist lands, is the harsh fact that the *Communists* control the distribution and these Bibles are chiefly for propaganda purposes and few ever reach the average citizen. Behind the contrived image of toleration of believers, children are being taken from Christian parents *for life* and put into atheistic boarding schools. Can you imagine the anguish of those parents who have had their children taken away?

Even as this spiritual struggle rages behind the Iron Curtain, as martyrs are dying for their faith, and as true servants of God are arrested and have their children taken from them for life, yet in the churches of the free world, one can go for years without hearing *one prayer* for our suffering brethren in Communist lands!

I have spoken around the world on behalf of the Underground Church and I have often asked, "Who here has prayed for the suffering Christians of the Underground Church?" Always the answer is almost no one!

It is a shame on the conscience of all free Christians. We from communist lands *are* your brothers and sisters in Christ. We are one body in Christ.

We ask for the Bibles and "tools of evangelism" we so desperately need to keep the Word of God alive.

The tragic lack of Bibles is the greatest need in the Communist lands today.

My people accept the suffering. They *understand* this is their cross.

But they *don't understand* why their brothers and sisters in the free world seem to have forgotten them — even in their prayers.

I am away from Ruth and the children speaking day and night now on behalf of the Underground Church and asking free Christians to pray for them.

It is our Christian duty before God to help the des-

157 •

titute, suffering families of men imprisoned for their faith. We must help them, and we have ways to do it.

I shall never forget how my own family almost starved when I was imprisoned. The same tragedy is now happening to many Christian families.

How can we sleep in peace at night, knowing the suffering they pass through? How can we read our Bibles and our hearts not weep for these who have no Bible?

The message I bring to you from the Underground Church is:

"Do not forget us."

"Pray for us."

"Give us the Bibles, the tools to work with, and we will use them for Christ."

I remember so well one of the dark solitary confinement cells at Persin. On the gray cement cell wall was a faded inscription scratched onto the surface by some unknown Christian who had been there before me. That inscription read: "HAS EVEN GOD FORGOTTEN ME?"

That anguished cry etched onto the prison wall is the cry coming from our fellow Christians of the Underground Church in communist lands today.

No, *God* hasn't forgotten them. And neither must we.

This is my message to you from the Underground Church.

If it is heard, and if my people receive the Bibles and help they need my years in Communist prisons will have been worthwhile.

Ruth joins me in this firm belief.

The author invites correspondence and gifts for the underground church as well as for printing of Bibles, to be sent to his address:

EVANGELISM TO COMMUNIST LANDS
P.O. Box 303
Glendale, California 91209